MARKETING
TO
GOVERNMENTS

By

CECIL V. HYNES

University of Maryland

and

NOEL B. ZABRISKIE

University of North Florida

TABLE OF CONTENTS

DOING BUSINESS WITH GOVERNMENTS

This chapter will orient the reader to the general nature of marketing to governments. Governmental buying units are unique when compared to either industrial or consumer markets and it is this uniqueness which helps to see the need for study of governments as a separate area of inquiry in marketing.

Marketing to governments is defined as the performance of those activities in a business firm which find, develop, and maintain contractual relationships with government institutions and agencies. Table 1-1 illustrates that in 1972, there were 78,268 basic governmental units which purchased goods and services. Each of these has anywhere from one to thousands of purchasing people. In large city, state, and federal procurement, these buyers will be responsible to or influenced by dozens of other interested parties who specify, legislate, evaluate, and use the goods and services involved in the transaction.

TABLE 1-1
Types of Governmental Units: 1962 — 1972

Type of government	1972	1967	1962
Total	78,268	81,299	91,237
U. S. Government.	1	1	1
State governments	50	50	50
Local governments	78,217	81,248	91,186
Counties	3,044	3,049	3,043
Municipalities	18,516	18,048	18,000
Townships	16,991	17,105	17,142
School districts.	15,780	21,782	34,678
Special districts	23,886	21,264	18,323

Source: *Government Units in 1972*, U.S. Department of Commerce, Preliminary No. 1, December, 1972, p. 1.

The opportunity to market to governmental agencies can change rapidly. Some of the important factors inducing change as well as some of the unique characteristics of government markets are discussed. Finally, the chapter provides an overview of state and federal government procurement which will aid in understanding the following chapters which detail the intricacies of finding and exploiting governmental selling opportunities.

GOVERNMENTS AS MARKETS

One of the early important principles that is impressed upon the student of marketing is that a unique marketing segment will require the firm to formulate a separate marketing plan to serve it. Another principle is that intensive study of the market segment is necessary before building the marketing program. These are also crucial rules for marketing effectively to governments.

Governmental markets include city, state, and federal institutional and agency procurement authorities. Large by any dimension, they represent great marketing opportunities and problems for firms. It is not governments that are sold to; it is their functional areas. In a major city such as Chicago, originators of buying situations include the police, education, highway, sanitation, and recreation agencies, to name a few. The state has comparable agencies that have similar needs but on a much larger scale. At the Federal level, important buying agencies include the departments of defense, space, interior, health, education, and welfare, postal service, and general services administration. In a strict sense, these are the places where an opportunity to sell exists, not to governments in general.

It is not unusual to go into a firm today and find separate sales managers for industrial, consumer, and government sales. Governments generally prefer to deal with manufacturers, although distributors do win some contract business.

There are many misconceptions about the relationship between business and government. Newspapers and magazines have given high visibility to problems such as the Lockheed Corporation's failure with the C-5A transport, and the cost-overrun of Gruman's F-14 attack bomber. At the state and city government level, the party out of political power exposes accounts of favoritism, excessive profits, and corruption in connection with contracts placed by the incumbents in office. These instances serve to justify the popular cynicism that marketing between firms and governments is generally corrupt. This generalization is unwarranted and does a disservice to the professional efforts of thousands of agency buyers, businessmen, and the elaborate systems of governments set up to assure equitable and honest contractual relations.

State and Federal governments are well aware that their buying procedures need improvement. The Council of State Governments reports that while most state governments have finally achieved a centralized buying capability, many practices need changing to improve state buying effectiveness.[1] At the Federal level, the Commission on Government Procurement created by Congress recommends major changes in buying to correct the inadequacies of current procedures cited by both government and business critics.[2] As governmental purchases get bigger and more involved with social issues, it is reasonable to expect that more problems in the government agency-supplier relationship will emerge and have to be resolved. With all of its problems, governmental markets are some of the most sophisticated in terms of legal and technical expertise and control checks to be found anywhere.

Government markets are different in a number of important ways from other markets. Some of their important characteristics include size of purchases, their transaction procedures, legal requirements, and rationale for buying.

UNIQUE CHARACTERISTICS

There are several dimensions to size of purchases. Size of an individual purchase by an agency or size of annual requirement by government level are two common frames of reference. The General Services Administration of the Federal Government can place one order for typewriters exceeding $500,000. To a supplier, such as the

TABLE 1-2
Selected General Expenditures by Governments: 1970-71

Expenditure a	All Government b	Federal Government	State Government	Local Government
Total Expenditures	$301,096	$177,922	$89,118	$94,797
Where Federal Purchases Predominate				
National Defense	80,910	80,910	——	——
Spare Research	3,334	3,334	——	——
Postal Service	8,683	8,683	——	——
Natural Resources	13,740	11,221	2,549	604
Housing and Urban Renewal	4,467	3,524	175	2,532
Air Transportation	3,176	2,185	189	914
Where State and Local Purchases Predominate				
Education	64,042	1,147	35,092	43,651
Highways	18,396	5,288	14,810	5,822
Public Welfare	20,446	11,986	16,278	7,870
Health and Hospitals	14,835	4,422	6,151	5,944

aExpenditures are function and represent $millions.
bDuplicative transactions between levels of government are excluded.

Source: *Governmental Finances in 1970-71*
Department of Commerce,
Bureau of the Census
GF 71, No. 5, P. 22.

IBM Corporation, this is a large order. On the other hand, the Defense Department spent $84.25 billion for goods, services, and manpower in 1970. Keep in mind however that this figure includes manpower costs. New hardware and research procurement is less than $84 billion. Aggregate buying power of these buyers attracts thousands of firms each year. Total expenditures by all levels of government was $332.98 *billion* in 1970, or in other words, approximately one-third of the entire gross national product of the country.[3] Government direct general expenditures in Table 1-2 illustrate the size and importance of purchases in government levels. Total state and local government purchases together almost equal the federal level, but are primarily spent on building and maintaining schools, health care, and roads.

Transaction procedures are frequently comparable to industrial marketing practices at the state and local level. Prospective sellers are qualified, required to be able to prove they can provide the need as specified, enter competitive bidding for a contract, and provide certification of performance. The person who decides that a need exists, the requisitioner, the buyer, the evaluator, and the user may all be different parties and be involved with the transaction.

The evolution of a government need is illustrated by the election of a governor. The new governor may have promised to ease traffic congestion in a populous part of the state during the election campaign. After election, he directs the legislature to sponsor and pass a bill to build the needed bridge. After extensive debate, the bill is passed and the Department of Purchasing is authorized to implement the statute. The specification is developed by the Department of Highways and qualified contractors are invited to bid on the project. After some negotiation, a bid is accepted and construction begins. In addition to the bidder's certifying performance at stages, highway engineers will frequently check on progress to assure that the bridge meets the specification. After several years of construction and testing, the automobile drivers happily begin using the bridge.

Who is the buyer in this case? Who must the marketer of cement, steel supports, or construction equipment design his marketing program for? The answer is often all of the directly involved parties who have decision power or influence.

At the federal level, opportunities to sell to the defense or space agencies become even more involved as numerous specialists and watchdog groups are added to assure that marketing procedures meet both the appropriate laws, the prevalent attitudes of Congress, and public critical opinion.

Federal government procurement is different from commercial transactions in other ways. Most of the buying agencies go to great lengths to *find* sellers and *inform* them on how to do business with them. While the government publications are too numerous to list, a few examples will illustrate that if a businessman wants to sell to a government agency, he must first contact the regional or national office and ask for documents such as these:

Selling to the Military, Department of Defense
Director of Private Programs Assisting Minority Business, U.S. Department of Commerce
Contractors Guide, U.S. Army Material Command
Research and Development Procurement, U.S. Air Force
Selling to the U.S. Air Force, Department of Defense
Commerce Business Daily, U.S. Department of Commerce
Handbook for Small Business, Senate and House Select Committees on Small Business
Selling to NASA, National Aeronautics and Space Administration

In addition to publications, governmental agencies hold seminars which orient businessmen to selling opportunities that exist and the procedures used by the particular agency.

While there are many such educational conferences during the course of a year, a typical example is the one held by the Small Business Office of the Space and Missile Systems Organization for 13 weeks in Los Angeles. The objectives were to encourage small businesses on the West Coast to seek government business and to educate them on how to do it.[4]

Non-government organizations also hold conferences to aid present and potential sellers. Throughout the year, Harbridge House, a Boston management consulting firm, and the National Defense Education Institute, an association of defense contractors, hold their meetings in different parts of the country to improve businessmen's knowledge of the ins-and-outs of government procurement.

Another major difference in *federal* procurement procedures is that if a seller does not like a decision by the buying agency, in some cases he can appeal it and get a review by the Armed Services Board of Contract Appeals. Seldom does a commercial marketer get an objective review if he loses an order or win a suit if he sues.

In many cases, government markets involve monopsonists. They are only buyers of bridges, roads, aircraft carriers, many types of research, and so forth. This can be a precarious selling risk for firms. The need for the product or service originates in authorizing legislation and a change of priorities by the executive or legislative branch can quickly end the need from the businessman. Cancellation of the support for the super-sonic transport was a disastrous blow to the sales of Boeing Corporation and the economy of the state of Washington. Accepting this risk, prudent marketers now carefully monitor their dependence on government originated orders.

The prospective marketer to government must first be completely familiar with legal requirements of the city, state, or federal agency that is to be dealt with. The basic procurement statutes and the major supporting laws are public and available upon request. In addition, a copy of the contract should be obtained and studied. Frequently buried in the fine print will be provisions which governments use to enforce other laws. For example, the federal contract may stipulate that the firm must employ a certain percentage of minority group workers, give preference in subcontracting to small businesses, and pay the minimum wage. These can make a dramatic change in the organization and policies of a business firm and cause it to decide that the cost of obtaining government business is too high.

Other legal requirements can make government contracts undesirable. The public nature of the bidding process may expose a firm's technology to competitors. If a bid is won, the firm is frequently required to expose highly confidential business information to government scrutiny, such as executive salaries, production processes and accounting procedures.

The objective of government buying is to obtain the specified product or service at the lowest possible price. This is modified to reflect other objectives important to agencies, such as boosting employment in some part of the country or maintaining the continuity of a firm's high technology capability. In defense procurement, a company can be awarded a contract because the buying agency believes a firm's management capability is better than other bidders even though its bid price is higher. There are limits to these other objectives and they are usually set out in the basic procurement regulation such as the federal government's Armed Services Procurement Regulation (ASPR) or Federal Procurement Regulations (FPR).

The large dollar volume of individual orders and aggregate purchases, transaction procedures, the number of parties involved in a transaction, the legal requirements for doing business with government agencies, and the public nature of the bidding process, are the most outstanding differences from commercial marketing. As the reader looks at the succeeding chapters, he will recognize that thus far, these differences cited are only summary statements. Establishing and maintaining a buyer-seller relationship is frequently much more involved than this, particularly in the bidding and negotiation procedures. The need for a continual liaison, the necessity for legal and accounting expertise, and the necessity to continually monitor the winds of change are other characteristics more important in government marketing than in commercial marketing.

WHY SELL TO GOVERNMENT?

To the uninitiated, the size of a government purchase alone might appear to be sufficient reason to seek orders from a city, state, or federal government unit. For standardized items such as desks, trucks, and paper, this would largely be true. High overhead costs of research and development are not involved. However, other reasons for seeking government business exist.

Marketers seek orders to utilize excess production capacity, to forestall competitors from getting the order, to assist in the cost of research technology that can be used on consumer or industrial products, or because they have a product which they believe to be superior to the one being used. There are dozens of reasons why a government order is sought and firms often have several motives for seeking a government contract.

On the other hand, there are many offsetting problems in realizing government business. A wry comment frequently heard among federal government marketers is that "the only thing worse than *not* having a government contract is *having one.*" The reasons for this attitude are many.

Government buying by state and federal agencies has become so complex that paper-work is choking the buying process. Many tiers of specialists and watch-dog groups monitor bidding and contract performance. This has proliferated in the last twenty years so that it is discouraging bidding by firms and the performance of firms with contracts. Businessmen complain about the voluminous forms, the slowness of response, and the high cost of obtaining government orders.

Contracts do not necessarily mean satisfactory profits. The federal government has a limit on the amount of profit that may be earned from a contract and has the power to renegotiate a contract to retrieve what it considers to be excess profitability. On the other hand, if a seller incurs losses in performing a contract, he may or may not be able to renegotiate the contract to retrieve the losses, or prevent further losses in continuing with contractual performance. Grumman Corporation is an example of how inflation, changes in requirements, and unforeseen technological development work have caused Grumman to lose $65 million on the production of the first twenty of the Mach 2, swing wing F-14, Naval fighter aircraft it built. The contract required the delivery of twenty-eight more aircraft and Grumman refused to build them until a new price was negotiated which would remove the $2 million dollar loss the firm was experiencing on each aircraft.[5]

The profitability of federal government orders is a matter of dispute. The Aerospace Industries Association reported in 1970 that

defense contract profits before taxes on sales were 4.3 percent
compared to durable goods non-defense sales which were 7.7 percent
in 1961.[6] But this may be misleading. The average return on invested
capital for aerospace contractors in the same year was reported to be
11.6 percent, which compares favorably with other industries selling
to the federal government.[7] Since more firms each year seek government orders, it is reasonable to believe that most firms achieve their
goals, profit or other reasons, to make it worthwhile.

The contracting procedure may make other changes in the firm
which has just won a government contract. The "motherhood"
clauses in the fine contract print will require the firm to comply with

TABLE 1-3
Selected Federal Requirements for Government Contractors

Requirement	Authority
Pay prevailing minimum wages.	Davis-Bacon, Walsh-Healey, and Service Contract Acts.
Report job openings to state employment agencies to aid job-hunting veterans.	Executive Order 11598
Refrain from discrimination in hiring because of race, reli-gion, sex, national origin, or age.	Executive Orders 11246, 11375, and 11141.
Provide performance bonds for payment of wages in certain circumstances.	Miller Act.
Provide "safe and sanitary" working conditions.	Service Contract, Contract Work Hours and Safety Standards, and Occupational Safety and Health Acts.
Refrain from contracting with companies convicted of crimi-nal violations of the Clean Air Act.	Clean Air Act.
Refrain from buying from cer-tain Communist-controlled areas.	Armed Forces Procurement Regulations.
Certify they comply with wage and price controls.	Economic Stabilization Act.

Source: *Business Week*, February 5, 1972, p. 46.

social legislation such as paying the minimum wage, equal opportunity, and buy America. Requirements which raise the cost of goods and trouble businessmen are shown in Table 1-3.

In 1971, Fairchild-Hiller Corporation lost a contract to General Electric Corporation. Fairchild charged that technical information from their bid was passed onto a competitor and requested that the General Accounting Office (GAO) review the decision. The GAO and NASA investigations resulted in awarding the contract to Fairchild.[8] This illustrates that it is possible for one of the many bid reviewers to leak confidential information to a competitor. Businessmen complain about this and the many ways that their knowledge and procedures are made public when they seek a government contract.

Despite these and othr reservations, hundreds of thousands of transactions are completed amicably each year.

There are barriers to entry into government business. A significant requirement is the great necessity to develop a total orientation to the statutes, processes, and attitudes of the people on the buyer side of the market. In high-technology goods and services, the necessity for sustaining high cost technicians while bids are evaluated can be a barrier also. The contract may be lost and the uncertain probability of winning the next opportunity creates a high risk business environment as Lockheed, Boeing, Westinghouse and other firms have found.

CHANGING OPPORTUNITIES

The election of a new executive or legislator frequently makes important changes in the opportunity for marketing to government. The new senators and representatives make campaign promises. The new governor says he is going to clean up the mess in the state department of highways. The new president is going to make the world safer to live in. After the oratory and inauguration, changes are made but not usually very swiftly.

Some trends in marketing opportunity seem to be dictated by whimsy. The Pentagon has a running five-year plan to strengthen the country's military posture, but when the Russians orbit a satellite, national priorities shift to space projects. The governor may intend to complete the interstate road system in a major city, but when 300 irate women appear at the executive mansion demanding day-care centers, a new priority has presented itself. The City mayor has plans for a new hospital, but when the black ghetto explodes into fire, riots, and gun-fire, new goods and services are needed. These events illustrate that government needs can shift dramatically and in some cases, quickly reorder priorities and therefore government needs.

The majority of marketing opportunities evolve slowly enough so that firms may enter and exit from government markets on an orderly basis. The safest markets are those that involve maintenance of existing programs. Supplying football uniforms to an educational system or liquor to service clubs on a military base can be as routine as many commercial marketing opportunities.

An intelligence system keyed strongly to all the influencers, deciders, and evaluators is more vital in government markets than in consumer or industrial markets. Continuous liaison is frequently the only way to become aware early of the winds of change. In this way, a firm can help to temper the loss of a contract, develop the capacity to seek additional contracts, or apply developed technology to commercial markets.

OVERVIEW OF THE BUYING PROCESS

It was stated earlier that the most important preparation a prospective seller can make in selling to a government unit is to first research the buying process of the unit. The following discussion will give the reader a general understanding of the state and federal buying procedures and establish a framework in which to understand the additional complexities introduced in following chapters.

Large city and state procurement procedures are similar; therefore only state and federal procurement processes will be presented.

State Buying Process

Most of the states have a centralized purchasing office to coordinate their purchases of goods and services. The purchasing by this centralized office parallels industrial marketing procedures to a great extent. There are some differences, however, because of both the dollar-value size of their purchases and the statutory requirements.

The process could be said to start when a state institution or department generates a *requisition*. This is a written form specifying the product needed. The requisition will either be filled from stock at the warehouse or will initiate the next step, the placing of an order with a supplier. This is true when a blanket order (or term contract) exists against which the buyer can periodically place an order either to replenish stock inventory or satisfy the needs of some state unit.

Assume that the need by the state unit is for a product not now purchased. This situation calls for the entire procurement machinery to be used.

After the requisition is created, specifications must be developed which provide good guidance to potential suppliers about what is needed, but not so detailed as to preclude a better product from becoming available, or limiting the number of potential bidders too severely.

If the need is for something highly technical, such as a new bridge or computer, a *Negotiation* bidding procedure may be used. Negotiation with suppliers is needed to refine specifications, arrive at an acceptable price, and in some cases, change the price after the goods are delivered when unforeseen contingencies warrant further discussion about price.

When the need is for well specified items such as desks or other less complex items, a *Formal Advertising* bidding procedure is used. The need is advertised to known suppliers and displayed in newspapers so that many firms can submit their bids for the contract. In both Negotiation and Formal Advertising, it is important that there are enough firms bidding to assure competition among potential suppliers.

The bids are opened at an appointed day and generally, the lowest bidder receives the contract. Goods will be inspected when delivered and after proper certification of the invoice, the firm will be paid.

Federal Buying Process

Federal needs for goods and services have many origins. Chapter III discusses the President as a major determinant of Federal spending. On a lower level, agencies and departments have routine needs for spare parts, maintenance of installations, and the support of programs begun in the past. It is appropriate here to outline the activities that are usually included in the term, procurement process. Procurement takes place when funds have been made available.

Prior to procurement, a need will have been recognized by some unit such as the Department of Defense or Transportation, or some other federal agency. While funds are being sought on programs necessitating research and development work, the procurement process can begin by doing the planning necessary to formulate specifications for the need. This would be true, for example, for a new bomber, types of space hardware or research, or an urban transportation system prototype.

When procurement begins, it will generally be either a *Negotiation* or *Formal Advertising* process. It is formal advertising if the need can be well specified in advance, and negotiation if development work is needed to translate a concept into products.

In both cases, a bidding package is prepared and enough potential suppliers must be attracted to assure competitive bidding. Extensive publicity is used in formal advertising and canvassing of known, capable suppliers is used in negotiation.

Bids are received, opened in the presence of all interested parties, and an abstract is made for any authorized party to see for several years after that day. In formal advertising, the contract will be given to the lowest *responsive* bidder. That is, if the purchasing official believes that the lowest bidder can't really perform what he says he can, the next higher bidder will be chosen.

In negotiation, a negotiation team will discuss and evaluate all bids with each bidder. A contract review board will evaluate the negotiation team report before the selection of a firm is made. After an agreed price is established, an *obligation* by the government will be created when both buyer and seller sign the contract. The successful bidder must verify he has met the requirements of the many clauses in the contract as he performs, and only after the appropriate technical group has assured the procurement officer that the received goods fully meet the performance agreement does payment get authorized.

The reader should not mislead himself into concluding from this quick view of the state and federal procurement processes that they are very similar. They are quite different in complexities, as will be pointed out in more detail in later chapters. At this point, it is enough to say that there are similarities in the use of terms, the professional attitude of the buyers, and in the acquisition of routine operating supplies. To appreciate some of the important differences and to lay an appropriate groundwork for discussing marketing to federal units, Chapter II discusses federal organization for buying and the scope of purchases.

SUMMARY

The opportunities for marketers to sell to state and Federal agency markets are huge by any dimension; the amount of dollars, firms, or the people involved. Furthermore, they are frequently complex in statutory requirements and procedures which require firms to fully implement the marketing concept in order to participate in the opportunities on a continuing basis.

Being large, the markets have imperfections as perceived by the firms, government personnel, and the media. State governments and Congress are aware of the imperfections and are striving to find ways to make the procurement process more efficient and fair to both buyer and seller. Chapter 10 discusses recommendations which may improve Federal procurement.

Government markets are unique in many ways in comparison to industrial or consumer markets. They make an effort to find and inform marketers how to sell to them, provide procedures for recourse if marketers feel they have been unfairly dealt with, and are supported by laws which detail the legal requirements of doing business with them.

The legal environment surrounding government purchases poses problems for marketers. Company information which can remain secret in commercial marketing must be exposed to government view in government contracts. Accounting and production information, salaries of executives, and product technologies are examples of privileged marketer information which may be scrutinized by government personnel in connection with contracts. Occasionally this information finds its way into the hands of competitors through leaks or procedures.

The risks associated with doing business with governments are sometimes formidable. Governments are the only buyers of some products and a shift in governmental priorities can cause a product market to diminish or disappear rapidly. Excess profits can be reclaimed from marketers and since governments implement social legislation through their contracts, if a firm accepts a contract without a knowledge of the hidden costs involved with modified business procedures, the risk of a negative profit is quite possible. An alert market intelligence system plus competent lawyers, accountants, engineers, and cost analysts are frequently necessary additions to the marketing organization of firms who want profitable contracts from government.

The chapter concludes with an overview of the state and Federal procurement processes to provide a preliminary understanding of the government buying situation. Following chapters will add more detail as the market environment is described and analyzed for marketer strategies.

FOOTNOTES

1. George W. Jennings, *State Purchasing*, The Council of State Governments, Lexington, Kentucky, 1969, pp. 90-105.

2. "A Plan to Centralize Government Buying," *Business Week*, December, 1972, p. 24.

3. *Governmental Finances in 1969-70*, U.S. Department of Commerce, Bureau of the Census, GF 70, No. 5, p. 22.

4. "18 Small Businessmen Take 13-Week Government Course," *AFSC News Review*, August, 1972, p. 7.

5. "Congressional Dogfight Over the F-14," *Business Week*, December 16, 1972, pp. 58-62.

6. *Risk Elements in Government Contracting*, Aerospace Industries Association, Washington, D. C., 1970, p. 1.

7. "Studies on Defense Contracting," *Harvard Business Review*, May-June, 1964, p. 26.

8. "NASA's Choice of North American Rockwell for Space Shuttle Detailed, Defended," *Wall Street Journal*, October 5, 1972, p. 12.

QUESTIONS

1. Explain some of the dimensions which justify calling government markets large and important.

2. In what ways do Federal agencies help marketers do business with them?

3. What are the ways in which government markets differ from commercial markets? What implications do these have for the firm who wants to seek contracts with either Federal or state government agencies?

4. What risks are inherent in winning a government contract?

5. What reasons do firms have for seeking government contracts?

6. Choose any major domestic or international event which has occurred in the last six months (such as an election, riot, flood, the SALT talks, passage of major law in Congress, etc.). Trace the event to the state or Federal agency that is probably involved with it. How will this probably affect government priorities, government purchases of goods and services, and the industries that may be involved. Does a marketer strategy suggest itself?

There are a great many opportunities for companies to sell their products to governmental agencies. These opportunities exist at both the federal and state level of government. However, there is more consistency in the organizational structure, operating procedures, and purchasing practices of the agencies at the federal level than at the state level.

Because the various fifty states have such diverse organizational structures and purchasing procedures, it would be impossible to cover them in the limited pages available. Consequentially, this discussion will be restricted to the major defense and non-defense agencies of the federal government that are responsible for procuring most of the products and services.

The marketing firm that desires to sell products to the federal government must understand how the agencies are organized, whether procurement is centralized or decentralized, and what types of products and services are used by the various agencies. The marketer will find that each organization has been established by law or governmental regulation and each is charged with purchasing certain specified products and services. Some of the organizations deal with general and common products, while others deal only with highly specialized products such as weapons systems for defense.

A small number of the agencies purchase products and services only at their Washington, D.C. offices, while others contract for such goods at many regional and branch offices. Often these branch offices are established in major industrial areas where the government will have a greater opportunity to contact large and small businesses in order to stimulate competition by marketers who wish to sell their products and services.

FEDERAL INFLUENCING AGENCIES

There are many government agencies that participate either directly or indirectly in the federal procurement process. In fact, all three branches of the federal government have some role to play in the procurement process. Congress enacted the legislation that governs the procuring activities; the executive branch is charged with the execution of the procurement process; and the judicial branch may be called upon to make decisions affecting procurement legislation, procedures, and actions. The procurement authority for the armed forces has been delegated by the President, the Chief Executive, to the Secretary of Defense.

Several different agencies within the federal government have a concern with the military procurement operations. These agencies do not get directly involved in the placing of contracts or the negotiations with regard to products. However, they do concern themselves with and influence the total procurement process.

Office of Management and Budget

The Office of Management and Budget was established in the Executive Office of the President by the Reorganization Plan of 1970. Among other things, the Office of Management and Budget assists the President in the preparation of the budget. The office reviews the military budget prepared by the Secretary of Defense and recommends changes as it deems appropriate prior to the time that the budget requests are submitted to Congress.

Office of Emergency Preparedness

The purpose of the Office of Emergency Preparedness is to assist and advise the President in coordination and determination of policy for all emergency preparedness activities. This office also determines the kinds and quantities of strategic and critical materials to be acquired and stockpiled against war emergency, under the Strategic and Critical Materials Stockpiling Act of 1946. It also consults with the heads of the various procurement agencies to determine whether procurement should be limited to domestic sources in the interest of national defense under the Buy American Act of 1933. It is also responsible for establishing policies, plans, preparedness programs, and readiness measures for the mobilization and management of the nations resources and production facilities in times of mobilization and emergency situations.

General Accounting Office

The General Accounting Office was created by the Budget and Accounting Act of 1921 and has been further extended by various other acts since that time. The General Accounting Office is directly responsible to Congress and generally has the responsibility of providing legislative control over the receipt, disbursement, and application of public funds. The GAO is under the control and direction of the Comptroller of the United States. The Comptroller General is responsible for prescribing principles, standards, and related requirements for accounting to be followed by the executive branches and agencies.

The General Accounting Office audits the receipts, expenditures, and application of funds by the departments and agencies of the federal government. It is charged with making independent examinations of the way in which government agencies are discharging their financial responsibilities. This includes examining the efficiency of operations and program management, determining whether government programs are achieving the purposes intended by Congress, and whether alternative approaches have been examined which might accomplish these objectives more effectively and more economically.

The GAO is also interested in examining the activities of those firms which have negotiated contracts with the government. It studies the activities of state and local governments, quasi-governmental bodies, and private organizations, in their capacity as recipients under, or administrators for, federal aid programs financed by loans, advances, grants and contributions. The GAO is also charged with recommending to Congress any changes in existing legislation which might be required to better utilize the resources of the government.

In the area of government procurement, the Comptroller General has granted to contracting and procurement officers the privilege of obtaining decisions on questions which arise incidental to proposed awards of government contracts. In addition, any bidder may request a decision on the legality of a proposed or actual award of a government contract adversely affecting him. These decisions are legally binding on the executive branch of the government. However, they are not binding on the congress or the courts. Thus with regard to procurement actions of the federal government, the GAO has principle functions of auditing, examining accounting procedures, settling claims, providing legal decisions on contracts and procurement actions, and examining management records and services.

Renegotiation Board

The Renegotiation Board was created by the Renegotiation Act of 1951 as an independent establishment in the executive branch of the government and was organized October 8, 1951 to administer the Act. The purpose of the Act was to eliminate excessive profits derived by contractors and subcontractors in connection with the national defense program. Thus, it is responsible for renegotiating defense and certain other types of government contracts to prevent profiteering. The Board operates through regional boards which have authority to conduct renegotiation proceedings within prescribed limits. The board furnishes renegotiation information to government procurement agencies when necessary, or appropriate, in furtherance of their procurement activities. If during the proceedings the board and the contractor are unable to agree upon the amount of excessive profits, if any, to be refunded by the contractor, the board then issues and enters an order determining such amount. The contractor then by petition may obtain a redetermination in the Court of Claims. The decisions of the Court of Claims are subject to review by the Supreme Court.

PURCHASING ORGANIZATION — DEFENSE

The constitution of the United States grants Congress in Article 1 the "power to raise and support armies." Military procurement gained formal status with the passage by Congress of the Purveyor of Supplies Act in 1795. This act served as the basic military procurement law until 1861 at which time the Civil Sundry Appropriations Act was passed. The Civil Sundry Appropriations Act, although set aside during both World War I and World War II, remained the basic law for military procurement until the passage of the Armed Forces Security Act of 1947 which unified the Army, Navy and Air Force under one statute. The 1947 law is the basic law controlling the Department of Defense (DOD) procurement. There are four basic organizations within the Department of Defense that purchase nearly all of the items for the defense of the country. These organizations are The Defense Supply Agency (DSA), and The Department of the Army, The Department of the Navy, and The Department of the Air Force.

The greatest percent of the military budget is spent for items of great value such as aircraft, missiles, ships, tanks, and other large pieces of hardware. Any of these items may cost as much as $25-50 million, and in total represent a large sum of money. Most of the purchasing activity, however, is related to the large number of spare parts, electronic equipment, and general purpose items that are required to insure the day-to-day operations of the various military units and bases.

The procurement of supplies for various military programs is conducted by the organizations listed above and in general follows four primary programs: 1) procurement done by each service for the various operations under their control; 2) procurement from a consolidated military source, such as the Defense Supply Agency; 3) procurement from other Government agencies and sources such as the General Services Administration; and 4) procurement for base operations from local sources of supply.

Defense Supply Agency

The Defense Supply Agency was established in October, 1961 and is directly responsible to the Secretary of Defense for providing supplies and services used in common by the Military Services. During the eleven years of its existence, the command of the agency has passed successfully from the Army, to the Navy, to the Air Force and is now headed by Lt. General Robinson, Jr., of the Marine Corps. The DSA as of June 30, 1971 was staffed by 1,081 people from the Army, Navy, Air Force and Marine Corps, plus 49,867 civilians.[1]

PURPOSE

The Defense Supply Agency provides logistic support to the operation forces of the Military Services in war and peace, and supplies some materials to Federal civil agencies. It operates in three main support areas. In *Supply Support*, DSA purchases, stores and distributes a large variety of items commonly used by the military forces and some civilian agencies. These items range from food items and clothing through construction equipment and industrial products.

The DSA provides *Logistics Services* by administering various programs for the Department of Defense. These include the Federal Catalog System, Material Utilization Program, DOD Coordinated Procurement Program, Research and Technology Information System, Surplus Property Disposal Program, Industrial Plant Equipment Reutilization Program, DOD Industrial Security Program, DOD-Wide program for redistribution and reutilization of excess government owned and rented Automatic Data Process Equipment.

The DSA provides *Contract Administration* services in support of the three military departments and other DOD components, National Aeronautics and Space Administration, other designated Federal and State agencies, and friendly foreign governments. These services include contract management, pre-award surveys, quality assurance, payments to contractors, support to small business and labor surplus areas, transportation and packaging assistance, mobilization planning, industrial security training and surveillance, reviewing contractor compliance with Equal Employment Opportunity regulations, and surveillance of contractor progress to assure timely delivery of high quality material and services.

ORGANIZATION OF DSA

The DSA headquarters is in Alexandria, Virginia. Headquarters is responsible for control over the field activities and the formulation of all policy. The field activities are located at strategic points throughout the country and consist of six Supply Centers, four

Defense Depots, four Service Centers, and eleven Contract Administration Service Regions. Each supply center is assigned the management of certain product categories such as food, clothing, medical, industrial, construction, electronics, chemicals and general supplies. For example, the Supply center for electronics is located at Dayton, Ohio; for construction at Columbus, Ohio; for Industrial equipment at Philadelphia, Pa.; for Personnel Support at Philadelphia, Pa.; for fuel at Alexandria, Va.; and for General services at Richmond, Virginia. The management of inventories is controlled by these centers except that fuel is only procured and not stored by DSA.

The defense depots are located in Mechanicsburgh, Pa., Memphis, Tenn., Ogden, Utah, and Tracy, Calif. These depots are responsible for the receipt, storage, and issue of supplies as directed by the Defense Supply Center having material management responsibility for the items involved.

There are four Defense Supply Agency Service Centers located in Battle Creek, Michigan; Memphis, Tenn.; and two in Alexandria, Virginia. The Federal catalog system, the defense surplus personal property disposal (sales) program, the Defense Integrated Data system, and a clearinghouse which helps the military services and other federal agencies achieve maximum use of supplies owned by the government, are all programs administered at Battle Creek. All records for controlling and disposing of Department of Defense owned, in use, and idle industrial plan equipment are maintained at Memphis, Tenn. All information pertaining to scientific and technical documentation and information is maintained at the Defense Documentation Center at Alexandria, Va. The Administrative Support Center at Alexandria, Va. provides administrative support to DSA and non-DSA activities, in accordance with interservice and interagency support agreements.

There are eleven Defense Contract Administration Service centers that manage contracts for the Army, Navy, Air Force, DSA, the National Aeronautics and Space Administration and other Federal and State agencies, and for foreign governments when properly authorized. Contract administration is a technical and administrative service supplied to the buying activities. Usually the service is performed at or near contractor plants to assure compliance with the terms and conditions of the government contracts. These regional service centers are located in Boston, New York, Philadelphia, Atlanta, Cleveland, Detroit, Chicago, St. Louis, Dallas, Los Angeles, and San Francisco.

OPERATIONS

The activities of the Defense Supply Agency have gradually diminished in the last two fiscal years which reflects the winding down of the Vietnam war. Many of the products and commodities handled by the Agency are closely related to the war effort. Other commodities, as shown in Table 2-1 are required for the continual operation of the Services and other government agencies regardless of whether we are involved in a war.

During the fiscal year of 1971, the DSA workforce was reduced by 7.7 percent and the level of procurement dropped to $3.5 billion as compared to $4.1 billion in 1970.[2] During fiscal year 1971, 18.6 million supply requisitions were handled by the Agency. In keeping with their policy of encouraging small businesses to bid on contracts, the Agency placed more than 44 percent of the dollar value of the 1971 procurements with small firms.

TABLE 2-1
Some Defense Supply Agency Commodities

Subsistence

Meat, poultry, and fish	Dairy foods and eggs
Fruits and vegetables	Bakery and cereal products
Coffee, tea, and cocoa	Nonalcoholic beverages
Food oils and fats	Sugar, confectionery, and nuts
Soups and bouillons	Condiments
Composite food packages	Jams, jellies, and preserves

Textiles and Clothing

Men's and women's clothing	Socks, undershirts and other knitwear
Wool, cotton and synthetic fabrics	Body armor
Boots and shoes	Dress and work gloves
Canvas products, tents and tarpaulins	Protective helmets and liners
Raincoats and other waterproof garments	Embroidered and metal insignias
	Decorations and badges
Hats and caps	Blankets
Flags	Wool tops

Medical, Dental

Drugs	X-ray equipment and supplies
Biologicals	Hospital furniture, equipment, utensils and supplies
Reagent grade chemicals	
Surgical, dental and opticians' instruments, equipment and supplies	Medical sets, kits and outfits
	Laboratory equipment and supplies

Fuel, Petroleum Products and Services

Gasoline and jet fuel	Operation of government-owned terminals
Fuel oils	
Coal	Commercial storage
Oils and greases	Aircraft fuel delivery service
Petro-Chemicals	

Electronics

Resistors	Switches
Capacitors	Connectors
Filters and networks	Crystals
Fuses and arrestors	Relays and solenoids
Circuit breakers	Coils and transformers
Electron tubes, transistors	Headsets and handsets
Semiconductor devices	Antennas and waveguides
Synchros and resolvers	

TABLE 2-1 (Cont'd)
Some Defense Supply Agency Commodities

Construction

Diesel engines and components	Warehouse trucks and tractors
Pipe and conduit	(self-propelled)
Hose and tubing	Conveyors
Plumbing fixtures	Power and hand pumps
Fuel burning equipment	Winches, cranes, derricks
Fencing, fences, and gates	Lumber and millwork
Vehicular power transmissions	Water purification equipment
Engine fuel system components	Gasoline engines
Vehicular furniture and accessories	Vehicular cab and frame components
Lubrication equipment	Electrical system components
Truck, tractor attachments	Brake, steering, and components
Plywood and veneer	Engine accessories

Industrial

Hardware	Chain and wire rope
Metal bars, sheets, and shapes	Rope, cable fittings
Blocks, tackle, rigging	Electrical wire and cables
Fiber rope, cordage and twine	Packing and gasket materials
Bearings	

General

Air conditioning equipment	Chemicals (non-medicinal)
Laundry and dry cleaning equipment	Insecticides
Shoe repairing equipment	Cooking, baking and serving equipment
Industrial sewing machines	Kitchen equipment and appliances
Mobile textile repair shops	Drums and cans
Materials handling equipment,	Ecclesiastical equipment
nonpowered pallets and skids	Rubber, plaster and glass fabricated
Ice chests, coolers, water dispensers	materials
and ice making machines	Scales and balances
Fans, air circulators and blower	Lighting fixtures and lamps
equipment	Drafting, Surveying and Mapping
Electrical hardware and supplies	Instruments
Woodworking machines	Liquid and Gas Flow, Liquid Level and
Geophysical and Astronomical	Mechanical Motion Measuring
Instruments	Instruments
Photographic film, paper and supplies	

Source: An Introduction to the Defense Supply Agency, U.S. Government Printing Office, Wash., D.C. 1972, pp. 8-9.

The Defense Supply Agency is responsible for maintaining the Federal Supply Catalog at the Defense Logistics Services Center, Battle Creek, Michigan. At the end of 1971 fiscal year, the Department of Defense items cataloged totaled 3,799,000. Of this amount, the Defense Supply Agency procures and manages 1.7 million items. In July 1971, the Logistics Services Center in Battle Creek started the construction of a building to house a new computer complex of the Defense Integrated Data System, which when finished is estimated to be the largest and most sophisticated data bank of logistics management information in the country. It is expected to integrate logistics management data on supply activities of the Defense Supply Agency, the Military Services and federal civil agencies. This data will be available to both management and user organizations through remote control terminals and high-speed communications.

Department of the Army

The procurement operations of the Army are for the most part the responsibility of the U.S. Army Material Command with head-quarters in Washington, D.C. This Command purchases all research and development for the Army and all materials used to support the combat mission.

Within the Material Command, there are various subcommands that have procurement activities in specific areas. The Army Missile Command in Redstone, Alabama buys rockets, guided missiles, ballistic missiles, and support equipment. The Army Munitions Command at Dover, New Jersey buys all ammunitions and war heads for the missiles.

The Army Aviation Systems Command in St. Louis, Missouri purchases all aeronautical and air delivery equipment plus any required test equipment or ground equipment for training purposes or maintenance of the air equipment. The Army Electronics Command located at Fort Monmouth, New Jersey procures all communications and electronic devices including test equipment, radar, fire control systems and data processing machines.

The Army Tank-Automotive Command at Warren, Michigan buys all tanks and related combat equipment plus all ground vehicles. This command is also responsible for design and development of new vehicles, improved maintenance procedures and monitors production of all land vehicles.

The Army Weapons Command at Rock Island, Illinois procures and manages all weapon systems including artillery weapons, aircraft weapons and related equipment. The Army Mobility Equipment Command in St. Louis, Missouri procures and manages surface transportation (other than tactical wheeled and general purpose vehicles), mapping and geodesy equipment, assigned electric power equipment, construction and services equipment, bridging and related equipment.

The Army Mobility Command also has procurement Agencies located in Chicago, Cincinnati, New York City, Pasadena, and Oakland, in addition to a depot system spread across the United States. The agencies listed above actually do much of the procurement of items used by the major commands of the Army.

The U.S. Army Corps of Engineers is responsible for contracting for military construction; maintenance, and repair of buildings, structures and utilities; and civil works such as river and harbor improvement, flood control hydroelectric power, public utility services and related projects. The main office for the chief of Engineers is in Washington, D.C. However, forty-nine district offices are located in major cities throughout the United States. Such offices are always listed in the yellow pages of the telephone directory.

Department of the Navy

The Navy Material Command has the responsibility of procuring and managing the logistic system for the Navy. The actual procurement is accomplished through functional commands and many decentralized purchasing operations. With headquarters located in Washington, D.C., the functional commands are: Naval Air Systems Command, Naval Ordnance Systems Command, Naval Ship Systems Command, Naval Electronic Systems Command, Naval Facilities Engineering Command, Commandant of the Marine Corps, Chief of Naval Research, Chief, Bureau of Naval Personnel, and Military Sea Transportation Service.

There are many purchasing Agencies and offices that operate under the direction of the various above commands. There are purchasing offices at the Washington Navy Yard, Brooklyn, New York, and Los Angeles, California. Navy Supply Centers and Depots are located at Norfolk, Virginia; Oakland, California; Great Lakes, Illinois; Charleston, South Carolina; Newport, Rhode Island; Seattle, Washington; Pearl Harbor, Hawaii; and Guam, Marinan Islands. All of the supply Centers and offices have procurement activities for general supplies, maintenance and supply items, and other items required by the various naval operations located near the supply centers.

The Naval shipyards and Repair facilities are located in Boston, Massachusetts; Bremerton, Washington; Charleston, South Carolina; Philadelphia, Pennsylvania; Portsmough, New Hampshire; New London, Connecticut; and Key West, Florida. Each facility procures general items as well as specialized equipment needed to operate the repair facility and rebuild the ships or special sections such as power plants or electronic navigation systems.

The Navy Aviation activities are handled through offices located at Philadelphia, Pennsylvania; Johnsville, Pennsylvania; Indianapolis, Indiana; Jacksonville, Florida; Pensacola, Florida; Cherry Point, North Carolina; and Corpus Christi, Texas. These operations procure all the specialized equipment, research and development, and repair parts necessary for equipping and maintaining all of the flying craft in the Navy.

There are ten procurement offices located at major cities in the U.S. that purchase all of the ordnance systems and supplies for the Navy. Items purchased are fire control systems, conventional ammunition, test equipment, electronic components, underwater sound equipment, and research and development pertaining to improvements in naval ordnance.

Contracts for naval construction projects and major station maintenance and repair are negotiated through regional offices located in Boston; New York City; Philadelphia; Washington, D.C.; Norfolk; Charleston; New Orleans; Great Lakes, Illinois; and San Juan, Puerto Rico.

The Navy purchases about one and one-quarter million repair parts and expendable items each year. This includes tires, office supplies, spark plugs, batteries, and other common-use items which are often purchased from small businessmen located in the areas of naval operational facilities.

Department of the Air Force

The Department of the Air Force is organized such that procurement is handled by three principal programs: (1) Systems Procurement, (2) Support Procurement, and (3) Base Procurement.

System procurement is done by the Air Systems Command with headquarters at Andrews Air Force Base, Maryland. It is responsible for the initial development of weapons systems for the Air Force. All missile systems, spare systems, communication systems, and new aircraft are initially procured through Air Force Systems Command's special procurement operations. Their offices are located at Air Force bases at Wright Patterson, Ohio; Norton Air Force base, San Bernardino, California; El Segundo, California; Bedford, Massachusetts; San Antonio, Texas; Muroc, California; Albuquerque, New Mexico; Valparaiso, Florida; and Arnold Air Force Station, Tennessee.

The procurement offices located above make the initial purchase and retain control of the production and delivery of each system and its component parts until such time as the particular system has been accepted by the Air Force, at which time all procurement responsibility is then transferred to the inventory managers at various depots across the United States.

Support procurement begins after the weapon or communication system has been accepted by the inventory depots. The support activities are under the direction of the Air Force Logistics Command at Wright Patterson Air Force Base, Ohio. The Logistics Command maintains procurement operations at San Antonio, Texas; Warner Robbins, Georgia; Ogden, Utah; Oklahoma City, Oklahoma; and Sacramento, California. Each of the above offices specializes in certain systems and commodities so there is no over-lap of procurement operations. All parts and supplies are inventoried by computer programs so that replacement parts can be purchased as needed for supplying the world wide operations of the Air Force.

Base procurement is performed by the 128 Air Force Bases in the United States. Hundreds of thousands of items are needed by the bases and most of these purchases are made through local business firms. Generally the items are of a commercial nature and are readily available on the open market. Local business men supply food items, maintenance and supply products, and do minor repairs at all U.S. Air Force bases. Each base maintains a procurement office staffed with contracting officers and other administrative people who make all the local purchases. Much of the procurement action is of a routine nature which can be handled easily following the small purchase regulations. All purchases totalling less than $2,500 for goods and $2,000 for construction, are accomplished through oral or written solicitation using purchase orders or blanket purchase agreements. This simplified system of procurement is adequate for the government and reduces the cost of operations at the base level.

FEDERAL PURCHASING ORGANIZATIONS — NON-DEFENSE

Many civil agencies and departments of the federal government purchase products or services as required by their day-to-day operations. Only those agencies that make substantial dollar purchases of products and services will be discussed in the following material.

General Services Administration

The General Services Administration (GSA) was established in July, 1949. It is much like a large corporation doing business in several unrelated activities. The GSA central office is responsible for five operating services, plus ten regional offices located in major cities throughout the United States. Table 2-2 gives a summary of the operations of the five operating services for the fiscal years 1962, 1971 and 1972. The activities of the Federal Supply Service doubled in the period between 1962 and 1972.[3] In Fact, with the exception of the defense materials operations, all service activities of GSA have increased. A brief discussion of each of the five services will provide some understanding of the volume of procurement carried on by GSA.

1. The *Federal Supply Service* of the GSA is responsible for purchasing items common to the needs of many federal agencies. In this way, it provides a consolidated purchasing, storing, and distribution network for the federal government resulting in substantial savings due to economies of scale from large quantity purchases. The

TABLE 2-2
Summary of operations
General Services Administration

	Fiscal Year 1972	Fiscal Year 1971	Fiscal Year 1962
Federal Supply			
1. Store sales (thousands of dollars)	522,075	478,469	264,379
2. Nonstore sales (thousands of dollars)	310,723	238,897	139,210
3. Stores line items shipped (thousands)	8,353.5	8,094.5	5,436.4
4. Number of supply distribution points	85	86	41
5. Total procurement (millions of dollars)	2,166.5	2,182.4	1,187.9
Property Management and Disposal			
1. Personal property (acquisition costs — millions of dollars):			
a. Transfers to other Federal agencies	920.1	751.2	362.7
b. Donations	419.8	399.5	350.7
c. Sales	70.4	74.6	39.8
Total	1,410.3	1,255.3	753.2
2. Real property (acquisition costs — millions of dollars):			
a. Further utilization of Federal agencies ...	174.0	12.0	97.0
b. Other surplus disposals (donations, etc.) ..	151.0	126.0	191.0
c. Sales	122.0	91.0	442.0
Total	447.0	229.0	730.0
3. Defense materials:			
a. Strategic and critical materials inventory (acquisition costs — millions of dollars) ..	6,088.2	6,257.9	8,686.6
b. Sales commitments (millions)	146.3	324.2	87.5
Public Buildings			
1. New construction program:			
a. Design starts (millions of dollars)	195.5	188.4	167.8
b. Design completions (millions of dollars) ..	571.7	280.0	196.7
c. Construction awards (millions of dollars)..	329.2	173.5	124.5
d. Construction completions (millions of dollars).................	142.3	49.4	149.9
2. Buildings management:			
a. Average net square feet managed (millions)	212.7	207.1	141.7
3. Repair and improvement:			
a. Repair and improvement appropriation:			
(1) Net square feet of R. & I. responsibility (millions)	139.6	187.8	128.5
(2) Obligations incurred (millions of dollars)	78.5	84.3	62.6
b. Reimbursable costs (millions of dollars) ..	79.1	64.8	N/A
Transportation and Communications			
1. Interagency motor pools:			
a. Number of pools in operation	98	97	66
b. Mileage (thousands)	635,195	583,565	249,571
c. No. of vehicles in pool (June 30)	60,816	57,213	24,359
d. Sales (millions of dollars)	67.7	57.2	20.9
2. Federal Telecommunications System:			
a. Number of intercity calls (millions)	109.0	87.6	N/A
b. Total system sales (millions of dollars) ...	176.8	153.5	N/A
National Archives and Records			
1. Number of records centers	15	14	16
2. Records in inventory (thousands cubic feet June 30)...........	12,758	11,229	7,864
3. Inquiries handled (thousands)	10,872	10,044	5,393

Source: *Annual Report,* 1972, General Services Administration, Washington, D.C., 1972, pp. 15-16.

supply Service operates eighty-five regional supply depots located so as to best serve the needs of government agencies in all geographical areas of the United States. The *Federal Supply Service* is a steady

market for thousands of common use items such as:
  Office supplies and equipment
  Household and office furniture
  Hand tools
  Refrigerators, Air-conditioners, and water-coolers
  Automotive vehicles and other motor-propelled vehicles
  Paint
  DDP magnetic tape
  Typewriters and other office machines
  Envelopes and stationery
  Maintenance and operating supplies and equipment
  Laundry equipment, safety equipment, plumbing and heating
    fixtures and accessories, filters, pipes
  Administrative equipment and supplies — printing, duplicating,
    and photographic equipment and supplies, sound recording
    equipment, packing and packaging materials, drafting and
    surveying instruments
  Firefighting equipment, ropes, medical kits, mess outfits,
    compasses, surgical dressings and material, lanterns, blankets,
    sleeping bags, and tents.

In some instances where the volume of orders for a particular item is either too large or too small to be handled efficiently through the depot system, the item may be purchased by indefinite quantity term contracts commonly known as *Federal Supply Schedules.* These *Schedules* are normally used each year and cover the purchase of more than 700,000 items such as automotive parts and accessories, tires, batteries, furniture, light bulbs, paper products, photographic and duplicating supplies, and athletic equipment.

Marketing firms interested in selling these products to the government should watch the advertisements for bids published in the Commerce Business Daily, local newspapers and on bulletin boards located in the General Services Administration's central and regional offices.

The *Federal Supply Service* has the responsibility for purchasing automatic data processing equipment and service for the Federal government. This presently represents a billion dollar business and is growing very rapidly. The Federal government is the largest single user of ADP equipment in the country and presently has 48 departments and agencies using 3,908 computers located in 237 cities throughout the United States. By one office handling the purchase of all ADP materials, the government gets the benefit of discounts given for volume business. Items purchased under this program are: major computer systems (hardware), software, services (data acquisition, conversion, computer time) support commodities (communications, peripheral equipment) supplies (cards, magnetic tape, forms);

replacement of obsolete equipment and the leasing of new ADP equipment.

2. *The Property Management and Disposal Service* has two principal responsibilities: (1) to manage the national stockpile of critical and strategic materials and (2) to dispose of excess and surplus supplies, equipment, and real property no longer required by the federal government.

There are presently ninety-two commodities worth $6 billion in the stockpile inventory, down from a high of $8.6 billion in 1962 when defense needs seemed more critical. There are seventy-seven different metals, minerals, ores and agricultural materials considered for stockpiling in order to meet the possible demands for such products in a war-time economy.[4] The *Service* contracts for storage space and equipment necessary to handle and maintain the inventories.

In its disposal operation, other governmental agencies may requisition surplus items before they are sold to commercial firms. Often personal property items are rehabilitated under contract by local business firms and the equipment is then reused by government agencies. Service contracts are currently in effect for the reclamation of valuable metals from used aircraft parts, i.e., platinum and silver from aircraft spark plugs and magneto points.

3. The *Public Buildings Service* acquires real property and constructs buildings for government use. The office of Design and Contracts procures the services of architects and engineers for new construction projects such as post offices, court houses, research centers, air conditioning systems, and repairs and improvement to old federal buildings. Construction contracts are awarded to the lowest responsible bidder utilizing the formal advertising procurement method.

This *Service* also leases general purpose space for federal agencies throughout the U.S. and Puerto Rico and the Virgin Islands. Leases are normally obtained through negotiation. This *Service* is also in charge of maintenance and repairs of government owned buildings. Cleaning supplies and repair items of a general nature are purchased by local offices from local businessmen. Most of these purchases fall into the category of routine small purchases, each totalling less than $2,500.

4. The *Transportation and Communications Service* (TCS) procures for GSA all transportation and communications services from commercial suppliers. Such procurement is usually done through the contract negotiation process. However, some purchases are accomplished by formal advertising. This *Service* operates the Federal Telecommunications System which is used by most federal

agencies. If an agency needs a special type of service, TCS may negotiate with firms to supply such service.

The Office of Motor Equipment of TCS operated in 1972 a total of 60,816 motor vehicles in 98 different motor pools.[5] This office purchases through *Federal Supply Service*, and contracts all motor vehicle parts and accessories, petroleum products, and repair services.

Through the Office of Transportation, TCS negotiates with transportation carriers all freight rates and services for all General Services Administration controlled shipments. This includes contracts for metropolitan drayage, for ocean shipments with ocean freight forwarders, and with firms for packaging, crating and marking.

5. *Selling to the GSA.* Any marketing organization that would like to sell products or services to the General Services Administration should contact the nearest regional business service center in regards to where to offer products and services. At the same time, the potential supplier should review the daily published lists in the "Commerce Business Daily" to see what products the GSA is interested in buying. A copy of the General Services Administration Stock Catalog and federal specifications would provide further information. And finally, the potential supplier should get on the GSA's bidders' mailing list for individual items that the firm wishes to sell the government. Many small businesses may participate in the GSA business opportunities because the GSA limits (some orders to small business competition only, and other times) will accept bids for small quantities of a larger order. These situations can be identified by working with the various regional offices of the General Services Administration.

Other Agencies and Departments

The supply needs of most of the small federal agencies are limited to office supplies, equipment, and other items that they get primarily from the General Services Administration. However, the following Departments and organizations purchase a large volume of varied and assorted products and commodities from business organizations.

1. *Atomic Energy Commission.* Procurement of products and materials for the atomic energy program is handled through thirteen field offices, each having nearly complete responsibility for the programs under its jurisdiction. According to budget figures, the AEC's expenditures for Fiscal Year 1971 were approximately $2.3 billion.

The *Field Offices* negotiate and administer contracts for the construction and operation of AEC-owned plants, laboratories, and other facilities. They purchase a limited amount of supplies.

The *Operating Contractors* who manage or operate the AEC-owned facilities do the major part of the purchasing that is done in the atomic energy program. They purchase supplies, manufacturing and operating equipment, and services that are required to operate the various plants.

Construction contractors purchase the supplies and equipment that is needed in the construction of the AEC-owned facilities.

Some of the other products and services purchased by the Field Offices are Architect-Engineering services; Management services; Fuel Processing, fabrication, and recovery services; Uranium concentrate; Basic research purchased by contracts that are granted on solicited or unsolicited proposals submitted to and approved by AEC in Washington, D.C.; and Applied Research and Development. Businesses interested in supplying the above services and products to the AEC should contact the Washington office for information on specific products required and location of procurement offices.

2. *Department of Agriculture.* The Department of Agriculture is responsible for a variety of programs and consequently purchases a great many different products. For the soil and forest conservation work, the department purchases earth-moving and other heavy equipment, such as tractors, graders, compressor, concrete mixers and cranes. It also purchases a substantial amount of construction materials, petroleum products, explosives, radio equipment, and surveying equipment, plus assorted tools and hardware items.

The department provides marketing and research services for the agricultural industry and consequently buys laboratory and testing equipment, such as microscopes, scales and balances, moisture meters, spectrophotometers, all types of farm and shop equipment, green houses and equipment, plus maintenance supplies for the various laboratories.

The Office of Plant and Operations has the general responsibility for all of the Department's procurement activities. Much of the procurement activities is conducted in the regional offices of the Department. Businessmen that are interested in learning of the marketing opportunities that exist for supplying the above products and services may contact the Department's Washington office and ask for a pamphlet entitled "Selling to U.S.D.A."

3. *Department of Commerce.* Nearly all purchases of administrative type products (supplies, equipment, and materials) used in the various office operations are made through a central procurement office in Washington, D.C. The specialized needs of the other major organizations at their central office locations. Businessmen interested in selling such products should write directly to the procurement offices of the Maritime Administration, National Bureau of Standards, Bureau of the Census, and the Environmental Science Services Administration. The Department will supply a pamphlet entitled "How to Sell to the U.S. Department of Commerce," which

contains a directory of the various purchasing offices and a list of the type of products most often purchased.

4. *Department of Health, Education and Welfare.* The Department purchases a wide variety of products and services for the many programs and staff operations in all areas of health, education, and general welfare programs. The greatest amount of dollar purchases are made for the operational programs related to the Public Health Service. Businessmen may secure information on the purchasing procedures and location of the decentralized procurement offices by contacting the Department at the Washington, D.C. office.

5. *Department of Transportation.* The various operational administrations and organizations within the Department have responsibility for procurements in their respective areas of interest. However, the Office of the Secretary of the Department does contract with consultants and other organizations for research and development studies covering the Department's various areas of responsibility.

The *Federal Aviation Administration* is responsible for air safety regulations; research and development of better systems, procedures, and facilities for air navigation and air traffic control; the location, installation, maintenance, and operation of visual and electronic aids to air navigation; management of the airspace and air traffic systems; plus airport planning and development programs. To carry out these functions, the *Administration* purchases equipment and supplies for aircraft, communications, air navigation and air traffic control fields. Major systems for air traffic control are purchased through the Headquarters office in Washington, D.C. Other equipment and supplies, plus construction contracts are procured through the various regional offices.

The *Federal Highway Administration* is involved in research and development studies for improvement of the controlled access highways, highway safety, and the testing of vehicles for improving safety standards. To carry out these and other activities, the *Administration* purchases automotive vehicles and repair parts, maintenance and support equipment and supplies, test equipment, and some types of road construction equipment. Businessmen interested in learning of the products being purchased should contact the Washington, D.C. office for information and to get on the bidders mailing list.

The *Federal Railroad Administration* contracts for research development and demonstrations for high speed ground transportation systems. It is responsible for railroad safety programs and for reviewing the economic operations of the various railroads with the responsibility of making policy for future operations and improvements of the railroad systems. Most of the purchases have been related to research and economic studies, plus in the last several years, a concentrated effort has been made toward the development of newer propulsion systems, vehicle control systems, and communications and guideways, for superior high speed ground transportation systems. Nearly all of the major procurement actions have been through the Washington, D.C. office.

Other organizations of the Department of Transportation such as the *U.S. Coast Guard*, the *St. Lawrence Seaway Development Corporation*, and the *Urban Mass Transportation Administration* purchase products and services that are required for their special functions.

6. *National Aeronautics and Space Administration*. The National Aeronautics and Space Administration was created in 1958 for the purpose of conducting research for the solution of problems of flight within and outside the earth's atmosphere, and develop, construct, test and operate aeronautical and space vehicles; conduct space exploration with manned and unmanned vehicles; arrange for the most effective utilization of scientific and engineering resources of the U.S. with other nations engaged in aeronautical and space activities for peaceful purposes; and to provide the widest practicable and appropriate dissemination of information concerning NASA's activities and their results. The Act which established NASA required that the regulations governing the military procurement activities be followed by NASA. Thus, the NASA Procurement Regulations are very similar to the Armed Services Procurement Regulations.

All NASA procurement activities are conducted by the twelve field installations. Each office solicits and negotiates contracts for the equipment and supplies necessary for its operations. It is also responsible for the procurement of research and development contracts for projects assigned to its installation. NASA buys some items from the General Services Administration, but primarily depends upon local businessmen for the supply of most operation and maintenance materials. Other outside organizations provide the scientific and engineering studies and development programs for each installation. Businessmen interested in selling products or services to NASA should write to the Washington office for information about the installation procurement field offices.

Business organizations, institutions, or individuals may also submit unsolicited proposals to NASA for research and/or development projects that will further the state of the art in space exploration or solve some particular problem. NASA has a formal procedure established for receiving and evaluating such unsolicited proposals.[6]

7. *Post Office Department*. The Post Office Department was created in 1970 as an independent establishment of the executive branch of the government. The major procurement activity is conducted by the Procurement Division located in the Washington, D.C. office. This office purchases special equipment such as postage

meters, stamp vending machines, cancelling machines, letterboxes, letter sorting machines, parcel sorters, sack sorters, bulk conveyor systems and monorail systems. Supplies of special types of inks, steel shelving safes, stools, lockers, cabinets, and pouch and bag racks are also procured through the central purchasing office.

The Post Office Department regional offices are responsible for procuring non-standard equipment necessary for a particular operation such as truck and trailer rentals, building and equipment maintenance supply items, and vehicle repair services. Most of the procurements are accomplished through the advertising and bidding process, with most of these products and services being supplied by local businessmen.

8. *Other Buying Agencies and Departments.* There are other independent agencies within the federal government which make some procurements, but the volume of business is not as great as in the agencies previously discussed. Such agencies as the Panama Canal Company, the Tennessee Valley Authority, and the Veterans Administration purchase products peculiar to their operations.

The Department of Interior purchasing operation is decentralized with the National Park Service, the Geological Survey, the Bureau of Commercial Fisheries, and the Bureau of Mines purchasing products necessary for their operations.

The Bureau of Prisons, the Federal Prison Industries, Inc., the Federal Bureau of Investigation, and The Bureau of Narcotics and Dangerous Drugs are all a part of the Department of Justice. Each of the bureaus is responsible for procuring the products and services required for its operations.

Most of the procuring activity for the Department of the Treasury is accounted for by the Bureau of the Mint, the Bureau of Engraving and Printing, and the Internal Revenue Service.

The purchasing procedure for the above agencies is much the same regardless of where the organization is located. Businessmen interested in supplying products or services to those agencies should write directly to their headquarters office for information or contact the local office of the agency. The local offices are always listed in the telephone directory.

SUMMARY

There are a great many opportunities for sellers to market their products and services to agencies of the Federal government. The seller must locate the buying agency that has a need for his particular product or service. Some agencies have decentralized their purchasing operations thereby making it easier to contact a greater number of sellers throughout the country.

All three branches of the federal government are involved in the procurement process. Congress enacts the laws, the executive administers the laws and regulations derived from the laws, and the judicial, through specific court cases, clarifies the laws and regulations.

Several federal agencies are involved indirectly in the military procurement operations. The Office of Management and Budget reviews the military budgets, and may recommend changes. The Office of Emergency Preparedness determines the kinds and quantities of strategic and critical materials to be stockpiled. The General Accounting Office, which is directly accountable to Congress, serves as a watch-dog over the expenditures of the departments and agencies of the federal government. It examines and audits procurement contracts if there is a question raised regarding the contract or the circumstances surrounding the contract. It also recommends to Congress any changes in legislation that would improve the utilization of government resources.

The Renegotiation Board was created in 1951 to review completed defense contracts to determine if the seller made excess profits. If the Board determines excess profits were earned, the seller must return the amount to the government. The Board's decision may be appealed by the seller to the Court of Claims.

The procurement for national defense is done through buying offices of the Departments of the Army, Navy, and Air Force, and the Defense Supply Agency. Each military service buys those special items needed to perform its mission. The Defense Supply Agency purchases the supplies and services used in common by the military services. The actual buying offices of the organizations are located throughout the country. Information on locations of buying offices and products they purchase is available from the headquarters of each organization.

The General Services Administration (GSA) is responsible for five operating services in ten regions of the United States. The Federal Supply Service purchases items common to the needs of many federal agencies. The property Management and Disposal Service manages the stockpile of critical and strategic materials and disposes of excess supplies, equipment and real property no longer required by the federal government. The Public Building Service acquires, constructs, and maintains buildings for federal agencies. The Transportation and Communications Service procures vehicles, communication services, and freight service for the agencies supplied by GSA.

Any marketing organization wishing to sell to the GSA should contact the nearest regional office for information or products and services, how to do business with the government, and how to get on the bidder's mailing list.

There are many other federal agencies and departments that

procure items for their operations. However, some of these organizations, such as the Atomic Energy Commission, the Department of Transportation, and the National Aeronautical Space Administration have special needs for research and development projects, and for products using complete technology. Sellers interested in those markets should contact the main office of such organizations to learn of their particular needs. There are many opportunities to sell products to the federal government, but the seller must take the initiative in locating them.

FOOTNOTES

1. *An Introduction to the Defense Supply Agency*, U.S. Government Printing Office, Washington, D.C., 1972, p. 4.

2. Ibid., p. 5.

3. *Annual Report*. General Services Adm., Washington, D.C., 1972, p. 15.

4. *Doing Business With the Federal Government*, U.S. Government Printing Office, Washington, D.C., 1970; p. 21 and *Annual Report*, General Services Administration, Washington, D.C., 1972, p. 9.

5. *Annual Report*, General Services Administration, 1972, p. 16.

6. The procedure is discussed quite fully in chapter 4. Unsolicited proposals are also accpeted by the Department of Defense and the military services.

QUESTIONS

1. What are the Federal agencies that influence and affect the procurement process? How do they affect it?

2. Why is the General Accounting Office responsible to Congress? What does the General Accounting Office do?

3. Discuss the purpose and operation of the Renegotiation Board.

4. What is the purpose of the Defense Supply Agency? How is it organized?

5. Does the organization of the Defense Supply Agency encourage small businessmen across the country to participate in supplying products to the Agency? Explain your answer.

6. How would a businessman determine which products the Army, Navy, and Air Force are interested in purchasing? What are some of those products?

7. Why are the procurement offices of the military services located in various parts of the country instead of at military headquarters near Washington, D.C.?

8. Discuss the responsibilities of the General Services Administration with regard to product and service procurements.

9. Discuss why the volume of activities by the General Services Administration has increased in the past decade.

10. Identify some of the other government agencies and departments that purchase special products and list their product interests.

THE FEDERAL PLANNING AND FUNDING PROCESS

3

In Chapter 1, a brief overview of the federal procurement process was discussed. That process frequently begins when funds have been apportioned to departments and agencies by the Bureau of the Budget. The funds are then allocated to the various subgroups within the agency or department so that they may begin procurement.

A knowledge of the sequence through which funds are appropriated and obligated can be a source of valuable information to the marketer to government. Specifically, it helps to: (1) estimate market trends, (2) furnish information for developing a marketing strategy, and (3) identify places where information can be gathered which will aid firms in responding to requests for proposals or invitations to bid.

Since the planning and funding process is eventually keyed to specific programs, knowledge of the origin of these programs provides a marketer not only a basis for pricing, but more importantly, a basis for product definition as well. By the time funds are allotted, they are tied to program elements which often go a long way toward describing the concept or product the customer is seeking. The use of a marketing intelligence system by a firm which can *continually* monitor the thinking of the people having decision authority over the programs and their elements is a key part of effectively marketing to the federal agencies and departments.

The Defense Department budget is by far the biggest among the federal agencies and departments. Perhaps for this reason, this budget has a highly elaborate planning, programming, and budgeting system through which the funding and purchasing of goods, research, and development are managed. All federal budgeting has approximately the same process, but the Defense budget is a good example since it illustrates the most elaborate system.

Government needs have many origins. Funding of existing programs such as a Naval aircraft carrier force, provisions for aircraft spare parts, repair requests, and maintenance of thousands of government installations are frequent entries into the National Budget. However, the President, as Chief Executive and Commander-in-Chief of the armed forces, is a key figure in influencing new government needs. The planning and funding process can be said to begin with the President and his *National Policies.*

DEVELOPMENT OF THE PRESIDENT'S BUDGET

The Defense budgeting process is comprised of a complex set of interlocking stages. The cycle of any one fiscal year is a continuous process dealing with past and present needs, as well as the needs of the future. This is visualized in Figure 3-1 as the first process of a two-part process; the planning and funding processes.

The planning process begins with the shaping of *national policy*. National policy considerations which the President greatly determines include the overall level of the national budget, the setting of priorities for government attention, and the balance between spending in the military and civilian sectors.

The national proiorities are partially indicated in the President's inaugural address, State of the Union messages, and press conferences. From these statements can be gleaned clues to the direction and strength of government effort. The comments of key congressmen are sought to get advance indication of any difficulty that key Defense Department projects might have when Congress holds hearings on the Defense part of the budget.

Trends in past defense expenditures are analyzed to find the clues to future needs. The slowing of the Vietnam war and stabilization of military spending is reflected in the decline in the Defense budget in recent years. In terms of 1972 dollars, the message is clear: $99.9 billion in 1968, $79.6 in 1971, and $76 in 1972. While certain armaments must be restocked, the message in the trend of decreasing expenditures is not lost on the prime and secondary contractors who supply Defense Department needs.

Shifting national policy is also evident in reports concerning the relaxation of military preoccupation with the Soviet land armies in western Europe, a shift of the greater armament load to other NATO nations, the closing down of overseas bases, and the Strategic Arms Limitations Talks (SALT) meetings.

The formulation of National Policy creates a basis for the President's National strategy. At this point, general programs are formulated to implement national priorities. The detailed planning documents in this phase are, for the most part, closely held and not available to the marketing community.

Defense Plans

Out of national strategy, the National Security Council sets basic military objectives. This involves the Secretary of Defense who works in turn through the *Joint Chiefs of Staff* (JCS) of the Pentagon. The JCS translate the objectives into tasks for the Navy, Army, and Air Force Departments. These military services then develop plans which

TABLE 3-1
The Planning Process: National Policies to the President's Budget

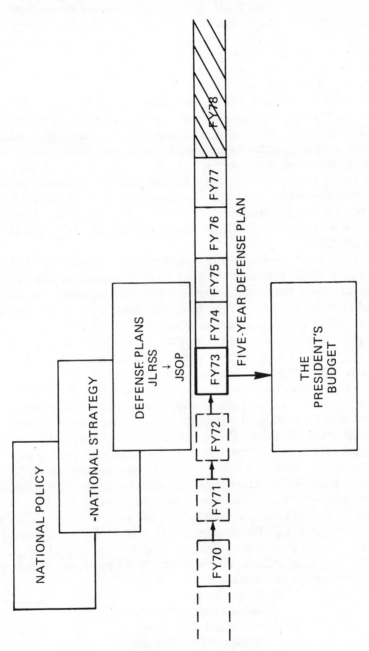

Source: Derived from the *Procurement Training Handbook*,
U.S. Government Printing Office, 1968, pp. 1-13.

will specify how they believe the task should be carried out, including the funding that will be necessary to implement them.

The Joint Chiefs of Staff annually prepare and revise three planning documents. The longest range document, the *Joint Long-Range Strategic Study* (JLRSS), covers a fourteen-year period *ahead* of the current fiscal year. The JLRSS involves strategic appraisal, concepts and strategies, and advice on research and development from technical support groups.

Derived from the JLRSS is the shorter *Joint Strategic Objectives Plan* (JSOP) which focuses on the first ten years of the JLRSS plan. Since it becomes more specific, it adds a layer of additional detail by clearly setting specific long-range research and development items, such as the need for missiles, bombers, Army missions, and Naval task force needs. Both the JLRSS and JSOP are documents setting out requirements, and while constrained by reasonable funding limits, they are not specifically constrained by budgetary limitations. These constraints are applied in the third plan, the *Five Year Defense Plan* (FYDP).

The FYDP becomes highly specific about program needs for the upcoming fiscal year and the four years following it. Military plans form the basis for determining research, development, and material requirements, and the FYDP translates these into budgetary needs for fulfilling the requirements. These are in the form of integrated programs that relate to one or more missions developed from the objectives. The FYDP is under constant review and changes reflecting shifting technologies, change in military concepts, and sudden international developments may initiate a *program change request* (PCR).

The political and marketing implications of a PCR are important. Initiation of a PCR by the Defense Department usually involves large systems such as ships, aircraft missiles, or other major weapons. Program changes of this size require extensive review, especially Congressional scrutiny. Since the PCR may require more funds, it comes under heavy attack from those military or civilian programs where cutbacks might occur and therefore whose funds are threatened. Marketers must carefully watch the movement of PCR's since they represent significant changes in the FYDP in terms of the creation, end, or important change of a government need.

The Five Year Defense Plan has nine major programs which constitute the nation's Defense plan:

I.   Strategic Forces
II. General Purpose Forces
III. Specialized Activities
IV. Airlift and Sealift Forces
V.   Guard and Reserve Forces
VI. Research and Development

VII. Logistics
VIII. Personnel Support
IX. Administration

There are approximately 1100 program elements under these nine major programs in which costs are detailed and annual funding is sought.

The President's Budget

The Department of Defense budget requests in any year are based on the first annual increment of the approved Five Year Defense Plan. Within this framework, the various military Services submit their annual budget estimates to their respective Defense Comptrollers. After the Secretaries of the Army, Navy, and Air Force approve the estimates, they are forwarded to the Secretary of Defense. Hearings and evaluations are made on each Services' budget and their relation to each other.

At this point, a single budget for the Department of Defense is formulated and submitted to the Bureau of the Budget. It reviews the estimates and their justifications, and balances the proposed budget for Defense against the competing estimates of non-defense agencies. Once this reconciliation is completed, all of the individual budgets are combined into the President's Budget document which will be submitted to Congress by January of each year.

FROM CONGRESS TO OBLIGATIONS

After the President's Budget is submitted to Congress, a period of extensive hearings by the House of Representatives and Senate begins. When both legislative bodies can reach an agreement on the fiscal year defense program, they authorize it by statute and appropriate funds. Generally, the Appropriations Acts of Congress provide no machinery to control the use of the appropriations.

It remains for the Executive branch to use the appropriated funds for the purposes set out in the statutes. However, Congress does stipulate the time limits for the use of the funds. The Appropriation Acts also stipulate the following stages of apportionment, allocation, allotment, committment, and obligation shown in Figure 3-2.

Apportionment and Allocation

Even after an Appropriation Act has been passed by Congress and signed by the President, funds become available only after the

TABLE 3-2
The Funding Process: President's Budget to Obligation

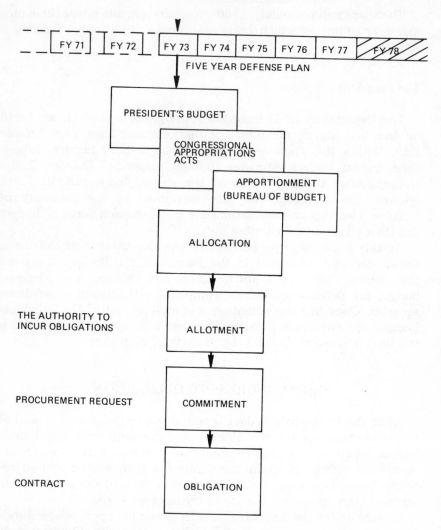

Source: Derived from the *Procurement Training Handbook*,
U.S. Government Printing Office, 1968, pp. 1-13.

Bureau of the Budget provides a release. *Apportionment* is a distribution by the Bureau of amounts available to each agency and department for spending.

In this case, the Secretary of Defense must also approve the rate of obligation. Together, the Bureau and Secretary provide an executive-level budgetary control. The apportionments are made on a quarterly basis during the year to avoid the need for a deficiency or supplemental appropriation. Thus, the apportionments become a management tool to insure that funds are fully expended and that obligations are not made for funds which have not been authorized.

Allocation is the further subdivision of funds to Departmental subdivisions. When an apportionment is received by the Department, the Department comptroller disperses the funds to the appropriate programs in the Department subdivisions.

Allotments to Obligation

Departmental sub-divisions may make allocations directly available for expenditure (obligation), or they may further sub-divide the allotments to program elements. An *Allotment* constitutes an authorization to incur obligations (a contract with marketers) within a specified amount of funds.

Commitment is a reservation of funds made by the official responsible for certifying the availability of funds. It authorizes obligations of funds without further certification. For example, when funds are committed against a procurement request, the contracting officer then has the authority to obligate the Government to a contract. This reservation of money is necessary because while goods may be ordered in 1973, they may not be paid for until 1974 or 1975 when they are received. The funds must be reserved for payment.

When a contract with a marketer has been created, then an *obligation* exists. As such, an obligation is a government liability resulting from a contractual agreement to acquire goods or services.

TIMING OF THE CYCLE

For the marketer, one of the most important aspects of the planning and funding cycle is the relation of the process to the calendar. For example, he knows that Fiscal Year 1973 funds will not normally become available on July 1, 1972, when the statute says it will, but rather, somewhere in the late fall of 1972. On the other hand, he also knows that some programs receive tentative resource allocations from the Secretary of Defense so that the planning for procurement can be well advanced by the time the money is available. Therefore, the marketing interface with government programs frequently starts well in advance of available funds.

Let us trace the timing through one cycle which takes approximately twenty months for preparation and enactment into legislation. In the fall of 1971, the Office of the Secretary of Defense passes down guidance to the military services for the 1974 budget.

This will be in line with the Five Year Defense Plan, but with last minute fiscal realities inserted, especially the President's desires about the size of the Defense budget.

By January, 1972, all of the military Services have augmented this guidance with detailed programs and their justifications. After considerable give and take among the Services, the Secretary of Defense sends the proposed 1974 budget to the Bureau of the Budget in late fall, 1972. By January, 1973, the Defense budget will have been reconciled with all other non-defense budgets and the President sends it to Congress.

From January to June, 1973, the Congress reviews, holds hearings, and takes testimony from the military Departments and Services. When the House and Senate reach an agreement, the Appropriations Act is passed and funds are approved. The period between July 1, 1973, when the funds are technically available, and late fall when they actually do become available, is occupied with the administrative processes of apportionment, allocation, and allotment.

The marketer who approaches an agency with a product in the fall of 1973 may not have much success that year because practically all of the funds are supposedly accounted for by planned programs. The marketing contact may have needed to be made in 1971 so that the product could become part of the budget planning process. Firms interested in selling products and services procured through Formal Advertising have less need to monitor this planning and funding cycle since these routine needs usually do not involve research and development work.

The next chapter will elaborate on the Federal procurement process which usually takes place after committment of funds occurs.

SUMMARY

Marketer activity to win a Federal contract often begins well in advance of the solicitation of bids discussed in Chapter 1. In order to be in the best possible position to respond to a request by a government agency, particularly NASA or the Department of Defense, marketers pay careful attention to the planning and funding activities of government that leads to market opportunities. This chapter discusses these processes in relation to the Department of Defense (DOD) as an example of one of the more complex sequences.

The planning process begins with the determination of national policies and goals by the President. The national strategy that is translated from these policies is developed by the DOD into programs or missions for each of the military services. The DOD has three levels of defense plans; the JLRSS for fourteen years ahead, the JSOP for ten years ahead, and FYDP for five years ahead. This latter plan is the most detailed by stating the weapon systems that should be continued or begun. The Secretary of Defense coordinates the planning of the Joint Chiefs of Staff and submits DOD's budgetary needs to the Bureau of the Budget, and executive agency to aid the President in submitting a budget request to Congress.

In January, the President's Budget goes to Congress for review and hearings. This will result in an Appropriations Act which authorizes the spending of government monies. This can be said to be the beginning of the funding process.

The funding process continues with a series of disbursements to DOD, then to the military services, and then to hundreds of defense program elements that will purchase the hardware and services that create military capability for missions. In government terms, this funding process is one of apportionments, allocations, allottments, commitments, and finally, obligations of the government represented by contract purchases. Most military weapons purchases are multi-year efforts with research and development contracts acting as a forerunner of contracts for hardware. Therefore, huge firms are most interested in those new programs submitted to Congress that will require new technology efforts. Other firms watch the budget to see if the program they are working on will be increased or decreased in funds.

A firm preparing to seek a contract must take cognizance of the timing of this sequence. Planning is well in advance of funding and therefore subject to change as international conditions cause revisions. Furthermore, money disbursements do not become available on July 1 as stated in the Appropriation Acts, but several months later as the monies are disbursed. These delay factors are part of the buying environment of federal markets which must be allowed for in selling strategies.

QUESTIONS

1. What advantages does a marketer gain by knowing the planning and funding sequence of the Federal government that results in bids and contracts?
2. In the case of the Department of Defense, who creates the need that results in market opportunities?
3. Marketers are not given access to long range planning involving the Country's needs for weapon systems. Where can clues be found elsewhere by marketers of potential opportunity?
4. Why are PCR's (Program Change Requests) watched with great interest by marketers and agencies of the government?
5. It takes three to five months for monies authorized by Congress to actually become available for spending. What implications does this have for marketer strategy?

FEDERAL PROCUREMENT PROCEDURES

Any marketing organization that wishes to do business with the Federal government should have a very good understanding of the procurement process used by the government. The professional buyers of the governmental agencies and departments must adhere to clearly defined and stipulated procedures. The Department of Defense and the Armed Services must follow the Armed Services Procurement Regulation (ASPR) when purchasing products and services. The National Aeronautical and Space Administration must be guided in its purchasing by the ASPR; and to a large extent all other agencies of the Federal government follow similar procedures.

In this chapter, we will first discuss the professional buyers who are responsible for procuring products for the federal government, and then discuss the basic methods used by the Defense sector and the civilian sector; namely, formal advertising procedures and contract negotiations.

PROFESSIONAL BUYERS

Procurement specialists who work for the government are normally well trained professional people. A person who is charged with the responsibility of committing the government to contracts worth millions of dollars is called a "contracting officer." He usually has a limited authority which is spelled out in a certificate that is provided him by his superior. His authority and responsibility has been delegated from the office above him. Only those professional people who have the proper experience, training, judgment, maturity, character, and integrity, and who understand the laws and regulations relating to the procurement process, are authorized to be contracting officers.

In the government procurement offices that purchase products for the Department of Defense and the military services, the contracting officers may be either military officers, or civil service employees. Regardless of their status, each must meet the professional standards as established by the governing laws and regulations.

For the past several years, the military services have been upgrading the positions of contracting officers by requiring that only college graduates be considered for such training. A degree in a technical area such as engineering, or business administration, or some combination thereof, is required. For those candidates selected as future contracting officers, the department of defense, either through its own facilities, or through the various military services, provides formal course work in purchase techniques. After the formal course work has been accomplished, a period of on-the-job training is required of each candidate. However, during the time of on-the-job training, the candidate may be given responsibilities with regard to certain procurement activities. For example, in the Air Force, the on-the-job trainees are second lieutenants who may have the responsibility of negotiating some small or non-complex contracts which may total several thousands of dollars in purchases. The on-the-job training, plus the opportunity to accept responsibility for contracts early in the training period, helps to develop the candidate's confidence with regard to his ability to interpret the various laws and regulations, and negotiate a proper contract. During this training period, the candidate is under the direction of a senior contracting officer and his work is normally reviewed to insure compliance with the many laws and regulations. During this time, the trainee gains experience and develops good judgment with regard to negotiation techniques.

The civil service trainees for the position of contracting officer also undergo a formal training period as well as on-the-job training. If the civilian trainee is going to work in a procurement office for one of the military services, or the Department of Defense, then his training is the same as that given to the military contracting officer. To be selected as a trainee, a person must have a college degree either in a technical field or in the area of business administration. The training is a very demanding process and it takes several years to become a proficient and effective contracting officer. Often the civil trainees start at a GS level of 9 or 10 which they maintain during their period of training. At the end of the on-the-job training, they then may be promoted to a GS 11 level where they start accepting the responsibility of negotiating all kinds of purchase contracts.

It is normally easier for the civil service to find qualified candidates for a contracting officer job than it is for the military. Once the civil service employee has acquired the necessary formal training and experience, he can then work productively in a procurement job with any agency or department of the federal government. The formal training helps to develop a clear understanding of negotiating techniques, laws and regulations that govern all procurement programs in the federal government.

In the procurement offices of the military services, military contracting officers and civil service procurement specialists work together in making the required purchases. For the many complex and involved procurement actions that the services use in procuring the major weapons systems, a contract officer may work as a head of the procurement team. However, in order to be certain that the procurement action is completed properly, he will have engineers and technicians working with him to make sure that the specifications are properly stated and that the bids as provided by the supplying firms comply with the specifications. Lawyers will usually be a part of the procurement team for they help prepare the invitations to bid or the formal requests for proposals that are submitted to the potential supplying firms. Lawyers also are required to review the contracts after they are written for legal soundness and to insure that the contract fulfills the requirements of the various laws and regulations. Many times, special negotiators, auditors, and price analysts are included as a part of the procurement team to insure that the contracts are reasonable with respect to costs and prices.

Prior to the award of major contracts, contract administrators or management people may be asked to review the contract and to determine the capabilities of the various contractors with regard to that specific contract. Later, after the contract has been awarded, management people are assigned to monitor the progress and performance of the contractor.

The contracting officer has a very important role to play in the procurement process. His professional attitude, training, and judgment are prime factors in maintaining the integrity of the government in its procurement actions. The contracting officer must recognize the problem of self-interest and integrity, and must be above reproach in performing his duties. He must maintain high personal standards and at no time accept gifts or gratuities or become involved in any kind of bribery. As a professional representative of the government, he is under constant scrutiny by the Congress, the press, and various members of industry, as well as the taxpayers.

FEDERAL PURCHASING
THROUGH FORMAL ADVERTISING

In procuring materials from private industry, the Department of Defense must follow the regulations established under the Armed Services Procurement Act of 1947. This act states that formal advertising is the preferred method of purchasing and should be used whenever the circumstances indicate it will be beneficial to the government. Under the formal advertising method, the government is assured of competitive bidding by those interested in selling a particular service or product to the government. Each bidder knows the specifications of the product or service to be purchased, has the opportunity to develop his own costs, and then present a bid, or price, based on his particular cost structures. Thus, the bids that are submitted for that particular contract reflect the cost structures of the various businesses submitting bids, and the government, by choosing the lowest bid, will normally be able to purchase the product at the lowest possible price.

The formal advertising procedures to be followed by a federal agency are established by the laws and regulations and the procedure cannot be changed by the individual agency that is making the purchase. However, the system is not so inflexible as to eliminate the possibilities of using good judgment in awarding a contract. Any variation from the statutory processes must be documented by the contracting office that has jurisdiction. The variation must be substantiated and documented, or else the contracting office may be charged with negligence in its procuring methods. The formal advertising process as set forth by regulations does avoid any problem of favoritism in awarding of contracts and helps to provide the integrity of the purchasing process for the government. Using this process, it is expected that the government will get the greatest value for the expenditure of public monies.

In order for the government to use formal advertising as a purchasing procedure, the agency that is making the purchase, or is responsible for doing the purchasing, must prepare specifications and a description of the item to be purchased. These must be in such detail that any company wishing to bid for this contract can determine exactly what product the government desires to purchase. They must be available to all firms wishing to bid on this particular contract and cannot be restricted for any reason.

In order to insure adequate competition among the bidders, at least two or more capable sources must be available to bid on a particular contract. In order to insure that there will be a sufficient number of bidders, the government purchasing offices maintain lists of firms that have an interest in supplying the kind of products normally purchased by that office. Such bidder lists are up-dated periodically. Companies that desire to have their name placed on the bidder list for any particular procurement office should complete a form provided by the government (see Figure 4-1).

When using the formal advertising process for purchasing, the government must be sure that sufficient time is available in which to publicize its specifications to those wishing to bid, and that those firms then have adequate time to prepare their cost figures and determine what bid they shall submit. The time allowed for this will vary, but normally it will not be less than sixty days. The process is slow, but it still ensures that all firms will be given the same opportunity, and that the government will fulfill its obligations in making purchases properly.

When making purchases based on the formal advertising method, the price of the product, or the bid price, becomes the sole criteria for determining who is the successful bidder. The law clearly states that the successful bidder will be the one who presents the lowest bid, providing he is otherwise qualified as "responsive" and

FIGURE 4-1

STANDARD FORM 129 JANUARY 1966 EDITION FPR (41 CFR) 1-16.802	BIDDER'S MAILING LIST APPLICATION	INITIAL APPLICATION REVISION

Fill in all spaces. Insert "NA" in blocks not applicable. Type or print all entries. See reverse for instructions.

TO (Enter name and address of Federal agency to which form is submitted. Include ZIP code)   DATE

1. APPLICANT'S NAME AND ADDRESS (Include county and ZIP code)   2. ADDRESS (Include county and ZIP code) TO WHICH SOLICITATIONS ARE TO BE MAILED (If different from item 1)

3. TYPE OF ORGANIZATION (Check one)   4. HOW LONG IN PRESENT BUSINESS

INDIVIDUAL   PARTNERSHIP   NON-PROFIT ORGANIZATION

CORPORATION, INCORPORATED UNDER THE LAWS OF THE STATE OF

5. NAMES OF OFFICERS, OWNERS, OR PARTNERS

PRESIDENT   VICE PRESIDENT   SECRETARY

TREASURER   OWNERS OR PARTNERS

6. AFFILIATES OF APPLICANT (Names, locations, and nature of affiliation. See definition on reverse)

7. PERSONS AUTHORIZED TO SIGN BIDS, OFFERS, AND CONTRACTS IN YOUR NAME (Indicate if agent)

NAME	OFFICIAL CAPACITY	TEL. NO. (Incl. area code)

8. IDENTIFY EQUIPMENT, SUPPLIES, MATERIALS, AND/OR SERVICES ON WHICH YOU DESIRE TO BID (See attached Federal agency's supplemental listing and instructions, if any)

9. TYPE OF BUSINESS (See definitions on reverse)

MANUFACTURER OR PRODUCER	REGULAR DEALER (Type 1)	REGULAR DEALER (Type 2)
SERVICE ESTABLISHMENT	CONSTRUCTION CONCERN	RESEARCH AND DEVELOPMENT FIRM

SURPLUS DEALER (Check this box if you are also a dealer in surplus goods)

10. SIZE OF BUSINESS (See definitions on reverse)

SMALL BUSINESS CONCERN*   OTHER THAN SMALL BUSINESS CONCERN

*If you are a small business concern, fill in (a) and (b):   (a) AVERAGE NUMBER OF EMPLOYEES (Including affiliates) FOR FOUR PRECEDING CALENDAR QUARTERS   (b) AVERAGE ANNUAL SALES OR RECEIPTS FOR PRECEDING THREE FISCAL YEARS

11. FLOOR SPACE (Square feet)   12. NET WORTH

MANUFACTURING	WAREHOUSE	DATE	AMOUNT

13. SECURITY CLEARANCE (If applicable, check highest clearance authorized)

FOR	TOP SECRET	SECRET	CONFIDENTIAL	NAMES OF AGENCIES WHICH GRANTED SECURITY CLEARANCES (Include dates)
KEY PERSONNEL				
PLANT ONLY				

THIS SPACE FOR USE BY THE GOVERNMENT   CERTIFICATION

I CERTIFY THAT INFORMATION SUPPLIED HEREIN (Including all pages attached) IS CORRECT AND THAT NEITHER THE APPLICANT NOR ANY PERSON (Or concern) IN ANY CONNECTION WITH THE APPLICANT AS A PRINCIPAL OR OFFICER, SO FAR AS IS KNOWN, IS NOW DEBARRED OR OTHERWISE DECLARED INELIGIBLE BY ANY AGENCY OF THE FEDERAL GOVERNMENT FROM BIDDING FOR FURNISHING MATERIALS, SUP-PLIES OR SERVICES TO THE GOVERNMENT OR ANY AGENCY THEREOF.

SIGNATURE

NAME AND TITLE OF PERSON AUTHORIZED TO SIGN (Type or print)

129-104

"responsible." *Responsive* means that the bidder must be capable of

FIGURE 4-1 (Cont'd)

INFORMATION AND INSTRUCTIONS

Persons or concerns wishing to be added to a particular agency's bidder's mailing list for supplies or services shall file this properly completed and certified Bidder's Mailing List Application, together with such other lists as may be attached to the application form, with each procurement office of the Federal agency with which they desire to do business. If a Federal agency has attached a supplemental Commodity List with instructions, complete the application as instructed. Otherwise, identify in Item 8 the equipment, supplies, and/or services on which you desire to bid. *The application shall be submitted and signed by the principal as distinguished from an agent, however constituted.*

After placement on the bidder's mailing list of an agency, a supplier's failure to respond (submission of bid, or notice in writing, that you are unable to bid on that particular transaction but wish to remain on the active bidder's mailing list for that particular item) to Invitations for Bids will be understood by the agency to indicate lack of interest and concurrence in the removal of the supplier's name from the purchasing activity's bidder's mailing list for the items concerned.

TYPE OF BUSINESS DEFINITIONS
(See Item No. 9)

A. MANUFACTURER OR PRODUCER means a person (or concern) owning, operating, or maintaining a factory or establishment that produces, on the premises, the materials, supplies, articles, or equipment of the general character of those listed in Item No. 8, or in the Federal Agency's supplemental Commodity List, if attached.

B. REGULAR DEALER (Type I) means a person (or concern) who owns, operates, or maintains a store, warehouse, or other establishment in which the materials, supplies, articles, or equipment of the general character listed in Item No. 8 or in the Federal Agency's supplemental Commodity List, if attached, are bought, kept in stock, and sold to the public in the usual course of business.

C. REGULAR DEALER (Type 2) in the case of supplies of particular kinds (at *present, petroleum, lumber and timber products, machine tools, raw cotton, green coffee, hay, grain, feed, or straw, agricultural liming materials, tea, raw or unmanufactured cotton linters*). "REGULAR DEALER" means a person (or concern) satisfying the requirements of the regulations (Code of Federal Regulations, Title 41, 50–201.101(b)) as amended from time to time, prescribed by the Secretary of Labor under the Walsh-Healey Public Contracts Act (Title 41 U.S. Code 35–45). For coal dealers, see Code of Federal Regulation. Title 41, 50–201.604(a).

D. SERVICE ESTABLISHMENT means a concern (or person) which owns, operates, or maintains any type of business which is principally-engaged in the furnishing of nonpersonal services, such as (*but not limited to*) repairing, cleaning, redecorating, or rental of personal property, including the furnishing of necessary repair parts or other supplies as part of the services performed.

E. CONSTRUCTION CONCERN means a concern (or person) engaged in construction, alteration or repair (including dredging, excavating, and painting) of buildings, structures or other real property.

DEFINITIONS RELATING TO SIZE OF BUSINESS

A. SMALL BUSINESS CONCERN. A small business concern for the purpose of Government procurement is a concern, including its affiliates, which is independently owned and operated, is not dominant in the field of operation in which it is bidding on Government contracts and can further qualify under the criteria concerning number of employees, average annual receipts, or other criteria, as prescribed by the Small Business Administration. (See Code of Federal Regulations, Title 13, Part 121, as amended, which contains detailed industry definitions and related procedures.)

B. AFFILIATES. Business concerns are affiliates of each other when either directly or indirectly (i) one concern controls or has the power to control the other, or (ii) a third party controls or has the power to control both. In determining whether concerns are independently owned and operated and whether or not affiliation exists, consideration is given to all appropriate factors including common ownership, common management, and contractual relationship. (See Items Nos. 6 and 10.)

C. NUMBER OF EMPLOYEES. In connection with the determination of small business status, "number of employees" means the average employment of any concern, including the employees of its domestic and foreign affiliates, based on the number of persons employed on a full-time, part-time, temporary, or any other basis during the pay period ending nearest the last day of the third month in each calendar quarter for the preceding four quarters. If a concern has not been in existence for four full calendar quarters, "number of employees" means the average employment of such concern and its affiliates during the period such concern has been in existence based on the number of persons employed during the pay period ending nearest the last day of each month. (See Item No. 10.)

COMMERCE BUSINESS DAILY

The Commerce Business Daily, published by the Department of Commerce, contains information concerning proposed procurements, sales, and contract awards. For further information concerning this publication, contact your local Commerce Field Office.

GPO : 1970 O - 408-271

producing the product as required by the government with regards to quality, reliability and delivery. *Responsible* means he has the financial base, production capacity, product know-how and willingness to perform. In all instances, the award of the contract must go to the bidder whose offer provides the greatest advantage to the government. This is where judgement may enter into the process, for if the low bidder is not determined to be responsible by the office making the purchase, then the next highest bid can be accepted.

However, such action must be justified in writing by the contracting officer involved.

If, at any time, any of the above factors cannot be present, then formal advertising will probably not be the most effective means for making the purchase.

Procedure for Formal Advertising Method

The first step in formal advertising is to prepare an "invitation for bid" ("IFB'S"). This invitation to bid spells out the specifications of the product to be purchased, the quantity of items, or the kind of service and the amount, the delivery schedule, any bonds or warranties required, inspection provisions, and other details pertinent to the purchase of this particular item.

These invitations are then sent to the firms on the bidders list, or any firm that has indicated an interest in having an opportunity to bid for this particular contract. At the same time, copies of the invitation to bid may be displayed at post offices or in the office of the purchasing agency, or at other public places. Many times, trade journals are used to advertise these invitations to bid, and often newspaper advertising is used. The Department of Commerce may also advertise the information regarding the invitation to bid in the Commerce Business Daily, which can be purchased through the government printing office.

Each invitation to bid includes a statement stating the specific place, date, and hour for the bids to be opened. It is then the responsibility of the bidding company to make sure that its bid is received in the proper place at the proper time so that it will be available for the bid opening procedure. At the specific hour for the opening of bids, all bids are publicly opened and read aloud. The company names and their bids are recorded and this information is available for public inspection. No company may withdraw its bid once the bids are opened unless there has been some mistake which is clearly recognized by the agency conducting the formal advertising process.

After the bids have been opened, each bid is reviewed by the contracting officers of the agency making the purchase to insure that the requirements of the invitation to bid have been met by each particular bidder. If it is found that a particular bid varies from the specifications in any manner set forth by the invitation to bid, that bid is then rejected. Under these conditions, a bidder whose bid is rejected is not allowed to submit another bid. It is at this stage of the process that the government ascertains whether or not the bidding company that is awarded the contract is, in terms of the government's needs, considered a responsible bidder.[1] If indeed the bidder is determined responsible, the contract is then awarded to that particular bidder. Thus, that particular bidder has in essence met all the provisions of the invitation to bid and his price has been found to be the lowest, or is fair and reasonable for the government.

As can be clearly seen by the above discussion, the process called formal advertising for purchasing is a time consuming and lengthy process. It requires a considerable amount of effort on the part of the bidding firms as well as on the part of the purchasing agency. Only certain products or services can be purchased using this method. However, it does insure that all firms who wish to sell products to the government have an opportunity to compete on a fair and reasonable basis. Under this process, the government can never be accused of impropriety and there should be no opportunity for collusion on the part of firms in trying to sell products to the government.

Two-Step Formal Advertising

The two-step formal advertising procedure was originally developed by the Air Force at the recommendations of the House Armed Services Committee. This method deviates slightly from the previously discussed formal advertising procedure. It is a method used primarily when the technical specifications are not clearly known at the time of the procurement action and thus cannot be clearly specified, as can be done in the invitation to bid.

Using this two-step procedure, the contracting office initiates action by requesting specific proposals from potential suppliers. These technical proposals are based upon specifications needed in the product to be purchased by the contracting agency. After the proposals have been submitted by the interested companies, the contracting agency and the company representatives discuss the technical aspects of the product. At this point, nothing is discussed with regards to price. Rather, the discussion centers around the technical suitability of the product being proposed by the potential supplier.

The second step of the two-step procedure is conducted on much the same basis as a formal invitation to bid, except that the invitations are restricted to only those firms that have been accepted as being usable by the contracting office. Each bidder must then submit his bid based on the technical proposal that has previously been discussed by the company and the contracting officer. After the bids are received by the contracting office, the contract is awarded to the lowest bidder. In order for this system to be workable, there must be enough interested bidders to ensure competition and each bidder must be fully informed with regard to the standards needed, along with other terms and conditions of the contract. The contract awarded is a fixed price contract, or a fixed price contract that has provisions for escalation at a future date.

The two-step method allows for flexibility in the formal advertising procedure, and gives the government an opportunity to explain and explore the technical requirements of the particular product that they are desiring to purchase. Thus it can often be used with new products or products that the government wishes to be improved, and yet keeps the benefit of competitive bidding.

THE NEGOTIATION PROCESS

All purchases made by the Department of Defense that are not made through formal advertising medias, are made through the use of negotiations in one way or another. Negotiation is a process that uses discussion and bargaining on the part of the contracting office to reach an agreement with the potential supplier on the prices and other terms of the contract being awarded. In no instance does negotiation mean that the government is limiting its purchasing action to one sole source for the procurement.

Negotiation is used on all procurement that is not made on a strictly price and competitive basis, but it does not necessarily preclude competition from ensuing. However, there may be cases where due to the special product to be procured, only one firm may be capable of supplying that product. Under this condition, it is then the responsibility of the contracting office to negotiate and bargain for the best possible price and quality of product for the government. Because of various built-in safeguards to the negotiation process, the government is able to determine the cost involved in producing a particular product and thus can readily determine, if necessary, whether or not excess profit has been made by the selling firm. In the following paragraphs, the negotiation procedure will be discussed in some detail so that a reader may gain a clear understanding of the advantages, and limitations, of negotiation as it is used by the government in procuring products.

When to Use Negotiation

The purpose of negotiation is to obtain the required products or services when and where they are needed by the government at reasonable prices. Negotiation is much more flexible than is the process of formal advertising. In the negotiation process, the contracting officer for the government has more latitude with which to use his personal judgment and professional knowledge regarding purchasing. Although rules and regulations determine to a large extent when and where negotiation will be used, there is still a great amount of flexibility left in the negotiation processes. Negotiation will most likely be used when there are fewer suppliers, or potential suppliers, of a given product or service. If the item being purchased is a non-standard item, that is there are no comparable commercial items on the market, then obviously negotiation is the proper procedure to follow in procurement. If the amount of the contract will be $2,500 or less, the law permits procurement by negotiation. However, if the contract to be used in the purchase is to be anything other than a fixed price contract, then negotiation is normally the best way to proceed.

The Armed Services procurement regulations as stated in title ten, of the U.S. Code, Section 2304, set forth seventeen circumstances when negotiation should be used in procurement.

Steps in the Negotiation Process

Negotiation is a procurement procedure used when flexibility in purchasing is necessary. In the Defense sector, regardless of which Department makes the procurement, the process is established by laws and regulations. Thus, a uniform negotiation procedure is followed by all military procurement organizations. The steps as listed in the ensuing discussion help to explain the negotiation procedure.

1. *Establishment of a purchase requirement.*—Before any action can be taken by the contracting officer of the purchasing office, the organization that will ultimately be using the item being purchased must establish the specifications of the item, and provide any other pertinent information relative to the production or procurement of the item. Many times, the specifications will be worked out in co-ordination with contracting officers. In the case of products where the technology is well defined, the specifications may be stated very precisely. However, in many instances where the product or hardware item being considered is expected to incorporate the latest type of technology in that area, the specifications may then be given in general terms, with the final statement on specifications being reserved until a later date after the negotiation process has been started between the contracting officer and the selling firm.

2. *Analysis by purchasing officer.*—In this step, the contracting officer or purchasing officer will look at the specification requirements for the particular item, and will make some judgment as to the type of contractual arrangement that would best be suited for the government in purchasing this particular item. The contracting

officer will review the technical specifications, the required time for delivery, the need for training of personnel, the need for handbooks, the need for stocking parts, and then judge where best to seek sources for this procurement. In most instances, the contracting officers are extremely able and experienced individuals, who have had experience dealing with similar products. Thus, based on that experience, they have some general conception of the type of procurement action that should be considered, as well as the firms that should be considered as potential suppliers for this particular product. In all instances, their efforts are directed towards writing a procurement action that will be best for the government.

3. *Request for proposals.*—After the contracting officer has reviewed the material provided him by the agency interested in purchasing the item, he develops a "Request for Proposals" which contains essentially the same information that would be given under the formal advertising procedure in the "Invitation for Bids." In most instances, the request for proposal stipulates the terms of delivery, the specifications of the product, the quantities to be purchased, and other requirements that must be met by the supplying company. After the request for proposal has been drafted, it is forwarded to the potential suppliers for that particular item or product. Usually the contracting officer sets a deadline of from thirty to ninety days for the submission of proposals by the various companies that have an interest in this particular purchase.

4. *Evaluation of proposals.*—At the end of the period allowed for the submission of proposals, each proposal received is thoroughly evaluated by the contracting officer to determine if it meets the specifications that were provided in the request for proposals. If it is clear that one proposal is substantially superior to all the others, then the government may begin negotiation with that bidder only. However, if it is deemed in the best interest of the government to negotiate with more than one bidder, then this procedure can be followed. In this instance, after some negotiation has taken place, each bidder is allowed to revise his proposal and try and meet the requirements established by the government through the negotiation process.

5. *Negotiation of the contract.*—This part of the procedure is really the heart of the purchasing process and is carried on over a period of time sufficient to allow an examination of all the pertinent facts to this particular proposal. If it is deemed in the best interest of the government, negotiation may be carried on with only one of the bidding firms. It is at this point in the process that the government

may require that the bidders supply them with cost data that has been used by the bidding firm in arriving at their proposal figures. Accounting procedures and technical information relating to the cost of production, as well as design of the item being considered, must be supplied by the bidding firm, if requested by the contracting officer. At this point, the contracting officer for the government is able to arrive at some judgment as to the reasonableness of the price of the item being purchased as well as the costs of the total contract. The contracting officer is interested primarily in ascertaining whether or not a reasonable profit will be made by the bidding firm on this particular contract, and whether the government is getting the best deal for its money.

6. *Award of Contract*—After the contracting officer is satisfied that the proposal has been reviewed and adequately negotiated with the representative for the bidding firm, the contract may be awarded to that firm. It is only after all questions have been answered, and all points of disagreement have been resolved that the award is made. At this time, it is assumed that this is the best contract that the government can get under the present circumstances.

The contract that has been negotiated now represents a legal agreement between the supplying firm and the government. The contract may be modified at a later date if both parties to the contract mutually agree. In many contracts, this procedure is accomplished because of a change in the state of art of the technology being used, or the government knows that it would be advantageous to make some changes in the product that is being manufactured. Whenever such changes are suggested by either party, a renegotiation process is instituted where both sides, or parties, discuss the implications of the proposed changes with regards to the original contract.

If the original contract that has been agreed upon by the contracting parties is to cover a period of time, say six months to several years, then a contracting office of the government maintains monthly reports that it expects the contracting firm to supply. The contracting officer generally follows very carefully the progress of the contracting firm. Milestones are established, or points in time, at which the contracting firm is supposed to either provide reports on its progress or supply certain parts of the item being produced. If it is determined at any time by the contracting officer of the government that the contractor or supplying firm is not meeting its obligations on time, or otherwise not meeting the time table established for the procurement of the product, then the government takes some kind of action to remedy the situation.

Contract Termination

If the government, in reviewing the actions of the contracting firm, finds that the contractor willfully failed to comply with the terms or conditions of the original contract, then the government may terminate the contract. Generally there is a default clause included in the contract stating under what conditions a contract may be broken, or terminated by the government, due to nonperformance by the contracting firm.

In many contracts, the government also includes the "termination for convenience" clause. This clause may be used any time that it is considered best for the government. This clause is usually invoked only when the contracted product is no longer of value to the government. Such might be the case if a particular piece of hardware for the armed services had been contracted for but was deemed no longer relevant for defense purposes. This particular clause may also be used to revoke a portion of the contract rather than the total contract.

If a contract is terminated by the government using this clause, the supplying firm is entitled to a settlement. Review boards are operated by the various services, such as the Air Force and Navy, to determine as much as possible a fair and equitable settlement for the action taken by the government. The settlement offered by the government may be challenged by the supplying firm. However, if the firm accepts the government payment, then that terminates that contract, or the portion of the contract, under consideration. Usually the supplying firm can negotiate a settlement with the government which is equitable to both parties. This situation however, points out the dangers that a firm may be facing when it signs a contract with the government to supply certain types of products used in national defense. The supplying firm if unwilling to accept the government settlement, may take the matter to the courts for a decision.

UNSOLICITED PROPOSALS — A MARKETER'S ADVANTAGE

If an organization, institution or individual has an idea or concept which he feels will be of value to the government, he may submit a proposal for the research and development of the idea. If the proposal has merit, a contract may be negotiated without regard to competition. Thus, the proposing organization has a marketing advantage which may be worth a substantial sum of money.

The Air Force Systems Command and the National Aeronautical and Space Administration are examples of agencies willingly accepting *unsolicited proposals* for research and development. These two agencies are both interested in innovations and ways of improving the state-of-the-art in their respective spheres of operations. In some instances, the proposed research may provide a specific solution to problems presently encountered, or it may help define problems of the future and then provide concepts or potential solutions for those problems.

If the unsolicited proposal contains proprietary data, or information, or an invention for which a patent is being sought, the government will not accept liability for failure to safeguard against open disclosures. However, the government office receiving the unsolicited proposal will take every effort to protect the information that is received. If the organization or individual wishes to restrict his proposal, he may mark the title page with the following information.

This data shall not be disclosed outside the Government and shall not be duplicated, used, or disclosed in whole or in part for any purpose other than to evaluate the proposal; provided, that if a contract is awarded to this offeror as a result of or in connection with the submission of this data, the Government shall have the right to duplicate, use, or disclose the data to the extent provided in the contract. This restriction does not limit the Government's right to use information contained in the data if it is obtained from another source without restriction. The data subject to this restriction is contained in Sheets _____.

Then on each page of the proposal which he desires to restrict he should have typed the following: "Use of disclosure of proposal data is subject to the restriction on the Title Page of this Proposal."

Research and development proposals may be submitted at any time. The best way of submitting the information is by letter. Included with the letter should be a very concise and brief statement of the proposed research and development. The governmental agency receiving the unsolicited proposal will acknowledge receipt of the proposal and thoroughly and completely evaluate it by appropriate personnel engaged in the technical areas that are comparable to that of the material submitted in the unsolicited proposal. Results of the evaluation will be forwarded to the orgranization that has submitted the proposal. In case the proposal is acceptable to the government, a contract will then be negotiated by the contracting officer of the proper agency in conjunction with the officials of the submitting organization. In the event the proposal is rejected, the government is in no way obligated to reimburse any organization or individual for costs incurred in submitting the unsolicited proposal.

CONTRACT AUDITS

A business firm with a federal government contract runs the risk of having the contract audited by the General Accounting Office. The General Accounting Office is an independent agency in the legislative branch of the federal government that serves as a watch dog over the executive branch for the Congress. In such a capacity, it audits the activities of executive departments and agencies. Thus it is concerned with the contracts that are negotiated and administered by the agencies, not necessarily to see if excessive profits have been enjoyed by the contracting firm, but rather to evaluate the management controls of the responsible agency.

The authority for making contract audits comes from at least five different laws.[2] Each law states the conditions under which an audit may be conducted. For example, the Armed Services Procurement Act (10 U.S.C. 2313 (b)) states:

> Each contract negotiated under this chapter shall provide that the Comptroller General and his representatives are entitled, until the expiration of three years after final payment, to examine any books, documents, papers, or records of the contractor, or any of his subcontractors, that directly pertain to, and involve transactions relating to, the contract or subcontract.

Not all contracts or subcontracts are examined. Some contracts may be audited because congressional committees or members of Congress want certain kinds of information pertaining to the contractors operations. Other audits result from information coming to the attention of the General Accounting Office regarding the contractor or the agency charged with managing the contract. For example, the information regarding a possible cost over-run on the Air Force contract for the C-5A was provided to the General Accounting Office prior to its thorough audit of the prime contract. In this case, the information was provided by an employee of the Air Force at the Joint Economic Committee's hearings on the Economics of Military Procurement. As a result of those hearings, Senator Proxmire requested the General Accounting Office to investigate the C-5A contract for possible cost over-run.

A subcontractor's operation may be audited to check on the management efficiency of the prime contractor with regard to the prime procurement contract. In such a circumstance, the audit provides Congress information on any excessive or unreasonable payments to contractors or subcontractors. In such an audit, the General Accounting Office reviews all books, documents, and records dealing with cost accounting data. It also examines all underlying data concerning the contractors pricing activity and plant operations, even though such data may not be *directly* related to the contract being reviewed.

During the last phase of the audit, prior to submitting its final report on the audit, the General Accounting Office discusses the findings with the contractor. The contractor can then present additional facts and data which he believes should be considered. The final report may absolve the contractor of any wrong-doing, but it may find short-comings in the way the government agency has managed the contract.

The final reports are addressed to the agencies having administrative responsibility for the contracts. Recommendations may be directed to the agency officials or to the Congress, depending upon the seriousness of the situation and the orders under which the audit has been conducted. A Congressional committee may direct the General Accounting Office to present recommendations that will serve to modify the basic laws governing that part of the procurement process.

SUMMARY

The procurement specialists who work for the federal government are well educated and trained professional people. These buyers are referred to as "contract officers" and may be members of the military service or hold a civil service position. The military services have their own schools and training programs for their contracting officers. To be eligible to train for these jobs, an individual must hold a degree in business administration or some technical field such as mechanical or electrical engineering.

The Armed Services Procurement Act of 1947 states that formal advertising is the preferred method of procurement and should be used whenever the circumstances indicate it will be beneficial to the government. Using this method, the government issues an invitation for bids stating the type of product and quality it desires, number of units to be purchased, delivery date, etc., and then normally accepts the lowest bid. Firms wishing to bid for these contracts should have their names placed on a bidder's mailing list or inform the buyers of their desire to participate in the bidding.

The two-step formal advertising method is used when the technical specifications of the product are not clearly known. Potential suppliers are asked to submit their proposals for review. The contracting officer and the seller discuss the technical aspects of the product. In the second step, invitations for bids are restricted to those firms that have submitted acceptable technical proposals. The contract is then awarded to the lowest bidder.

Negotiation is used on all procurement actions that are not completed by the formal advertising method. It is most beneficial when procuring a non-standard, special product, or complex system, and there are few potential suppliers. The success of negotiations for the government depends on the knowledge, experience and judgment of the professional buyer.

In the negotiation process, the customer or user specifies as clearly as possible the product it needs to solve a given problem or perform a certain mission. The purchasing officer will analyze the users needs and determine where best to seek sources for the procurement. Next, "requests for proposals" are sent to potential suppliers stating what mission is to be accomplished and, if possible, the specifications of the product. The interested seller submits his proposal stating what product he can supply that will meet the needs of the user. Then the contracting officer and each potential supplier discuss the firm's proposal. Finally the contracting officer selects one proposal as best, and a price and contract is negotiated, after which the contract is awarded to the winner.

The government may terminate a contract if it is judged to be in the best interest of the government. However, the seller is reimbursed for the work he has done on the contract. Review Boards are maintained by the military services to insure equitable treatment of the sellers. If the seller desires, he may take the case to the Courts for a final decision.

The military services and the National Aeronautical Space Administration will accept unsolicited proposals from firms interested in doing special research and development projects. The projects must be relevant to the needs of the service or NASA. If the proposal is accepted, a suitable contract is negotiated.

Contract audits are conducted by the General Accounting Office which is an independent agency of the legislative branch of the government. The audits are to evaluate the management controls and actions of the responsible agency. Both prime and sub-contracts made by the various procurement agencies may be audited. Besides reporting its findings, the General Accounting Office may also be requested to submit recommendations to Congress for modification of the basic procurement laws.

FOOTNOTES

1. Responsible bidder as defined on p.

2. Budget and Accounting Act 1921 (31 U.S.C. 53); Budget and Accounting Procedures Act of 1950 (31 U.S.C. 67); Armed Services Procurement Act (10 U.S.C. 2313 (b)): Federal Property and Administrative Services Act (41 U.S.C. 254 (c)); Atomic Energy Act (42 U.S.C. 2206); and the Anti-Kickback Act (41 U.S.C. 53).

QUESTIONS

1. Describe the characteristics an individual should possess to be a good contracting officer.

2. What are the responsibilities of a contracting officer?

3. Explain the formal advertising method of procurement.

4. How does the two-step advertising method differ from the old formal advertising method?

5. Why was the two-step method developed?

6. What is meant by a "responsive" bidder?

7. What is meant by a "responsible" bidder?

8. Describe the various steps in the negotiation process.

9. Why is negotiation a more flexible method of procurement than the formal advertising method?

10. How does the "request for proposals" differ from the "invitation for bids"?

11. Under what conditions might the government terminate a contract?

12. When is an "unsolicited proposal" accepted by the Air Force?

13. What is the purpose of a contract audit?

14. What agency is responsible for making contract audits? Why that particular agency?

CONTRACTS AND THE BUYING PROCESS   5

For all Federal government purchases other than those classified as small purchases, i.e., one single transaction of less than $2,500 for supplies, or construction contracts of less than $2,000, some type of contract is used. In fact, governments at all levels, federal, state, county and city rely upon contracts as the basic agreement between the buyer and seller. Most government procurement, regardless of the level of government, is based on public law which usually establishes guidelines for the contractual arrangements. The selling firm must understand these procurement laws or it will be at a disadvantage during the negotiation process. The seller must also understand the various contracts, and make sure that the contract he signs will give him a reasonable profit and that his obligations are clearly stated. If he submits a low bid on a contract and it is accepted, he has to produce the product or service at that price or face prosecution through the court system.

CONTRACTS

The discussion in this section will concentrate on the contracts developed by and used by the Federal government with the greatest emphasis placed on those contracts used in the Department of Defense and the National Aeronautical and Space Administration.

Federal government procurement represents the greatest outlay of funds and the largest number of procurement actions of any level of government. Consequently, it has had considerably more experience developing and using contracts than any other procurement organization. The contracts vary from the simple to complex. However, they are representative of the types used at all levels of government.

BASIC PROVISIONS OF CONTRACTS

Procurement activities by the various government agencies, other than the purchase of small supplies, result in a contractual relationship between the government agency and the supplying firm. These contracts are the basic form of communication between the buyer and seller and as such are of primary interest to both parties. These contracts often reflect the results of long and intense negotiation during the procurement process. Because the agencies purchase so many different and varied types of products and services, each contract must be tailored as much as possible to fit the specific needs of that procurement action.

Each contract written by the government agency contains specific provisions that govern the performance of both the procurement agency and the supplying company. These specific provisions are worked out during the negotiation period. However, in addition to the specific provisions, most government contracts contain general provisions that must be followed by the supplying firm. These general provisions as stipulated by law are published as a part of the Federal Procurement Regulations, and as such, are made available to each firm that is a party to a government contract. A complete statement of the general provisions is provided in the Appendix.

Each supplying firm must meet the requirements of the general provisions which cover such problems as variations in quantities, inspection requirements for products, payments to the seller, assignment of claims, actions to be taken in the case of default, actions with regards to disputes, patents, information on the Buy-American Act, Walsh-Healy Public Contracts Act, information on contingent fees, and other subjects that have a significant bearing on the performance of the supplier. Copies of these general provisions are provided to the bidding firms or supplying companies in standard form so that all participating firms are fully aware of what is required.

In the past, most of the procurement was done on a formal advertising basis with the resulting contract being a fixed-price contract. However, as the complexity of the products increased and the unknown quantities regarding technological development became apparent, it was necessary to find other types of contracts that would provide the flexibility needed to accommodate both the interests of the government and those of the contracting firm.

All government agencies generally recognize that profit is a basic motive of the business enterprise. Profit, per se, is not the only motive for business. However, it is necessary if the enterprise is to survive over a period of time. Thus, many businessmen look upon profit in much the same manner as they do material, labor, overhead, and general and administrative expenses, all considered elements to be covered by the price of the product in the long-run. Adequate profits as envisioned by the contract, are generally in the best interest of the government, if in fact, the government's objectives with regard to the contract are achieved.

During the sixties, the Department of Defense and the National Aeronautics and Space Administration working together devised ways of introducing incentives into the contractual arrangement. This was done by modifying and changing the basic concept of the contract so that it reflected incentives to motivate the seller to earn more compensation by achieving better performance and controlling his cost. Thus the purpose to incentive contracting was to motivate the seller to a performance which is in the best interest of the customer, in this case, the government agency. This is accomplished by adjusting the seller's profits in proportion to the value (to the customer) of the actual completed contract performance in comparison to target profit and performance goals expressed in the contract. The seller is then primarily involved with the motivational aspect, while the government is concerned with the value it receives for a better performance. The underlying philosophy to incentive contracting is that to the degree that a seller can be motivated by profit to produce more efficiently, he is achieving the government's objectives.

TYPES OF CONTRACTS

Because of the variety and volume of supplies and services that must be procured by government agencies, different types of contracts must be used to provide some degree of flexibility in procurement actions. Generally, there are two basic categories of contracts, *fixed-price contracts* and *cost-reimbursement contracts.* Fixed-price contracts are written stating a price for full payment of the work when the product or service meets the standards established by the contract, and the product or service is delivered by a specified time.

Cost reimbursement contracts are characterized by an agreement between the buyer and seller, where the buyer agrees to reimburse the seller for all allowable costs necessary to perform the service or produce a product.

The firm-fixed-price (FFP) contract is at one end of the continuim with the seller assuming full cost and profit responsibility, while the cost-reimbursement contract, usually referred to as cost-plus-fixed-fee (CPFF), is at the other end where the seller has a minimal cost responsibility and little motivation to control costs and thus increase profits. Between the two extremes of the firm-fixed-price and the cost-plus-fixed-fee contracts are variations of the two categories which include several incentive type contracts currently being used.

The *incentive type contract* is used to provide incentive to sellers to reduce costs and increase or improve performance. During the negotiation process, standards are agreed upon by both parties which are then used to evaluate the performance of the contractor after the completion of the contract. If the evaluation committee or board decides that the seller reduced or has controlled costs effectively, has given good performance, has met delivery dates, or has surpassed expectations in other areas of contract performance, the fee or profit for the seller may then be increased. The increase is based on a pre-agreed upon sharing formula which determines the amount of increase due the seller. On the other hand, if the seller has failed in his performance on the contact, the same formula determines how much will be reduced from his profit. The complexity of the particular procurement involved will be considered when establishing the standards of performance applicable to the contract. The complexity of the procurement will also determine the type of incentive contract that will be used, or tailored as much as possible, to fit the specific circumstances.

Fixed Price Contracts

Procurement regulations state that the firm-fixed-price contract is the most preferred type because the seller has greater profit motivation, and he accepts full cost responsibility. However, this type of contract may not always be the right contract for certain procurement actions. To provide flexibility for this type of contract, certain variations have been developed which are discussed below.

1. Firm-Fixed Price Contracts—(FFP). In an FFP contract, the price is agreed upon by the buyer and seller before the contract is awarded and that price remains in effect for the life of the contract, unless revised pursuant to change clauses in the contract. For the seller, this type of contract provides the greatest risk as well as the maximum potential for profit. If costs are greater than those estimated by the seller when signing the contract, he will lose money on the contract. However, if his operation is more efficient than he expected, he may actually earn a much greater profit than he originally estimated. This type of contract is easily administered by both the government and the seller. Such a contract is well suited for procurements of standard commercial items or military items where specifications are well defined, price competition exists, costs are predictable, and production capability is known to the buyer.

2. Fixed-Price Contracts with Escalation.—This type of contract is usually used when the fixed-price contract extends over a long period of time and when costs of raw materials, component parts, and/or labor may change. Because such future cost increases cannot be reasonably estimated at the time of the contract award, provisions are included to "escalate" the price upward and downward when specified contingencies occur. This type of contract may be used in the formal advertising method of procurement as well as in procurements based wholly on the negotiation process.

3. Fixed-price Incentive Contracts with Firm Target—(FPIF). The purpose of this type of contract is to show the seller that he will benefit from sound management and a reduction in the costs of producing or delivering a product or service to the buying agency. Such a contract (FPIF) stipulates a target cost, target profit, target price (usually target cost plus target profit), price ceiling, and a sharing arrangement agreed upon by the buyer and seller. After completion of the contract, the actual costs are compared to the target costs and any costs over (or under) target costs are shared jointly by the buyer and seller in accordance to the agreed upon ratio. For example, if the cost-sharing ratio of 70/30 were negotiated, the buyer would benefit by a decrease in cost to the extent of 70 cents of each dollar and the seller would increase his profit by 30 cents. However, for each dollar of costs above the target cost, the buyer would pay 70 cents and the seller 30 cents. Regardless of the sharing arrangement, the buyer will never pay more than the price ceiling stated in the contract. Thus, if costs are exceedingly high, it is conceivable that the seller could perform the work at a loss. The sharing arrangement should always reflect the degree of cost responsibility required and the incentive necessary and consistent with the circumstance surrounding a given contact. Under certain circumstances, the buyer may have to go to a 50/50 or better sharing arrangement in order to provide the proper incentive for the seller.

4. *Fixed-Price Incentive Contract, Successive Targets*—(FPIS). This type of contract is designed for procurements where long lead times may make it necessary in the acquisition of a new system to contract for future follow-on quantities before adequate cost and pricing information is available. In some instances, design and production stability has not been achieved at the time of the contract and thus an FPIF contract cannot be negotiated. However, adequate cost and pricing information will be available at a point in time relatively early in the performance of the follow-on contract. In such a situation, the FPIS contract will have successive cost targets and determinations established. By the time the first unit is delivered, the FPIS contract should be finalized providing for a ceiling price and a sharing arrangement reflecting the uncertainties that will exist during the life of the contract.

5. *Fixed-Price Contracts with Prospective Price Redetermination*— (FPRP). This type of contract provides for fixed prices to be used in a prospective period. Thus a series of two or more firm fixed-price contracts may be negotiated at stated intervals during the performance of the contract. The buyer and seller negotiate an initial FFP contract based on the best cost data available at that time, agreeing that at some specified time in the future, determined as a date or percentage of performance, they will adjust the price in accordance

with data available at that point in time. This type of contract has been used in the area of aircraft engine procurement.

6. *Fixed-Price Contracts with Retroactive Price Redetermination*—(FPRR). The Armed Service Procurement Regulations limit the use of this type of contract to small dollar, short term contracts for research and development. It provides for adjusting contract price after performance (completely retroactive), subject to a ceiling price that is negotiated initially, using audited contract costs as a basis for the price revision.

Cost Reimbursement Type Contracts

Cost-reimbursement type contracts indicate an arrangement between the buyer and the seller whereby they agree upon an estimate of the contract costs which the buyer will reimburse the seller from time to time, for allowable costs necessary to get the work done. Reimbursement may be full or partial according to the specific agreement written into the contract, and it may, or may not include a provision or payment of a profit (fee). The Federal agencies use at least five different cost-type contracts which are briefly discussed below.

1. *Cost Contracts*—(CR). With this type of contract, the Government agrees to reimburse the seller for all allowable and allocable costs incurred in the performance of the contract, but no profit (fee) is paid. The costs that are allowed are those costs determined in accordance with the ASPR or NASA regulations and any specific provisions of the particular contract. Inasmuch as no profit is allowed, this type of contract is used primarily for research contracts with educational institutions or contracts providing physical facilities to contractors.

2. *Cost-Sharing Contracts*—(CS). Under this type of contract, the buyer agrees to reimburse the seller for a predetermined portion of the allowable and allocable costs of the contract performance. This type of contract is designed for research and development procurements. If used for other than educational institutions or foreign governments, the ASPR stipulates that conclusive evidence must be shown by the contracting officer that the seller has a high probability of receiving substantial present or future commercial benefits from the project. A company's willingness to share costs should not be a factor in source selection, nor should the acceptance of such a contract place the seller in a preferred position in competition for future contracts of any kind.

3. *Cost-Plus-a-Fixed-Fee Contract*—(CPFF). When using this type of contract, the buyer agrees to reimburse the seller for all allowable and allocable costs incurred in performance of the contract, plus a

specified number of dollars above the cost as profit (fee) for doing the work. The fee is negotiated by the buyer and the seller. This contract is designed primarily for use in research or exploratory development when the level of the seller's effort required is unknown, work specifications cannot be defined, and the uncertainties of performance are so great that a firm price or incentive arrangement cannot be agreed upon during the life of the contract. Under this contract, the seller has little reason to minimize costs or manage the work effectively. Because of the possible abuse and high costs of procurement when using this type of contract, the government has decreased the use of CPFF contracts, using it primarily for developmental work. Once the technology has been identified and there is a high probability that development is feasible, the government can then determine its performance objectives and completion schedules, and then negotiate new contracts based on price incentive measures.

4. *Cost-Plus-Award-Fee Contract*—(CPAF). This contract is a variation of the CPFF contract discussed above. It is used primarily in the procurement of technical services, such as design, programming, engineering, and R & D work. During the negotiation process, the parties agree upon a minimum and maximum fee that can be earned and a set of criteria by which the seller's performance will be measured and evaluated. The seller's work is periodically evaluated by a Government board set up under the terms of the contract which determines the amount of award fee to be paid to the seller representing an incentive payment for efforts extended by the seller during that period.

5. *Cost-Plus-Incentive-Fee Contracts*—(CPIF). This contract is a cost-reimbursement contract with the added feature of an incentive sharing formula for profit (fee) for the seller. Under this contract, there is no ceiling price established, allowable and allocable costs are reimbursed in accordance to ASPR Section XV, and the maximum profit the seller can receive is subject to ASPR limitations (in development contracts, 15 percent of target costs; production contracts are limited to 10 percent). Generally both maximum and minimum profit levels are negotiated under a CPIF contract. Thus after a project reaches the target cost level, the seller will receive a minimum profit, even though the costs may eventually increase above the target level. The CPIF contract is used in procurements for advanced engineering, or operational systems development and first production, where the uncertainties of performance preclude the use of a fixed-price-incentive type of contract. Crucial to the success of this type of contract is the negotiation of the target cost and the incentive sharing formula. Target cost must be a realistic figure arrived at by the best judgment of the parties. The probabilities for overrun should not be greater than the probabilities for underrun and

the share formula should give the seller the proper incentive to control costs.

Time and Material Contract (T-M)

Under this contract, the buyer and seller negotiate a price for the time (labor-hourly rate) and the buyer agrees to pay for all materials used at cost. The hourly rate includes direct labor, overhead and profit for the seller. This contract is generally used in situations where the amount and duration of the work cannot be predicted, such as engine overhaul work or other maintenance work. No profit is allowed on the cost of materials because to do so would violate the prohibition against cost-plus-a-percentage-of-cost contracting. A particular disadvantage of this contract is that the more time the seller takes to do the job, the greater the contributions to his overheads and profit.

Letter Contract

A letter contract is defined in the Armed Services Procurement Regulations as "a written preliminary contractual instrument which authorizes immediate commencement of manufacture of supplies, or performance of services, including, but not limited to, preproduction planning and the procurement of necessary materials." This type of contract is used by the Department of Defense and National Aeronautics and Space Administration when time is critical and it is necessary to get a seller started immediately on some project. It may also be used when there is some administrative delay or problems in negotiations with respect to the major contract, yet it is deemed important to get the seller started while the problems are being resolved. In any event, a letter contract must be replaced by a definitive contract within 180 days or upon completion of 40 percent of the contract performance, whichever occurs first. The use of letter contracts has been discouraged because the Government is at a disadvantage in negotiating the final contract once the seller has started work on the project.

DETERMINING WHICH CONTRACT TYPE TO USE

There are several important factors that must be considered by both parties during the negotiation process when determining the type of contract for a given procurement action. These factors are the incentive approach to be used, the uncertainties of contract performance, the environment, the seller's accounting system, and the negotiation process.

The Incentive Approach

The use of incentives to motivate the seller to control costs and provide a better total performance is based primarily on the importance a seller attaches to profits. The government is most interested in using a contract type under which the profit a seller earns will vary inversely with the costs of performance. Thus if the seller can reduce costs and improve his performance on a contract, he will be able to increase his profits by a pre-determined amount. Conversely, if he fails to control costs, he will realize a reduction in profit from the total contract. The use of an incentive type contract reminds the seller's managers that day-to-day decisions regarding alternative courses of action will have a bearing on the ultimate cost of the contract and be directly reflected in the profit to be earned at the completion of the contract.

While most incentive contracts are concerned with cost control, there may be other situations where special incentives can be used to attain other important objectives. Such objectives might include a better performing system, more reliable product, earliest possible delivery, or improved products through the use of value engineering techniques. When such a situation exists, both parties to the negotiation process should carefully evaluate the various kinds of incentives available and then select the one or ones which will have the greatest chance of success, given the complexity of the procurement action being considered.

Uncertainties in Performance

Contracts are written at the present time covering future development, production, and delivery of products or services. The longer the prospective period covered by the contract, the greater the number of variables that are injected into the situation, and the less reliable are the estimates regarding these variables. For example, a long period of time between the award and first delivery of the product may mean a high degree of design, tooling, and prototype engineering, and testing is required. This may result in uncertainties that were unanticipated during the negotiation for the award of the contract.

The negotiated price at the time of the award must be based on, and justified by, all available cost and price data submitted by the seller. However, the terms of the contract reflect the best intelligent interpretation of the data presented and are based on the realistic judgment of the negotiators regarding what should happen in the future. If the design of the product has not been stabilized, then clearly there will be some degree of performance uncertainty. If the product is not comparable to other products that have been produced, then comparative price analysis is extremely difficult and the use of prior production experience is very limited.

As a program progresses from research through successive stages until a product is in the production stage, increasing amounts of cost and support data become available. To offset the uncertainties in performance, it is often advisable to use a cost-plus-fixed-fee contract for the research and development stage of the project. Then as the design is stabilized and cost data is available regarding the production process, a new contract, such as a firm-fixed-price contract might be written.

Contract Environment

In selecting the proper contract type, including the incentive and sharing arrangement, there should be a complete understanding of the physical and contractual environment at the place where the seller will perform the work. Regardless of the contract type used, if the dollar amount is small ($50,000), compared to the average monthly billings of the seller ($2 million), that contract will probably receive a minimum of management attention. At the same time, if the product being manufactured is a simple or standard product, it will undoubtedly receive just routine management consideration regardless of the amount involved, expecially if the firm has had considerable experience with past production runs.

Accounting System

Before the parties to the negotiation can settle upon a particular contract type, it is important to determine whether or not the seller's accounting system will permit timely development of the necessary cost data required by the contract. This may be particularly critical when a fixed-price-incentive successive targets contract is going to be used. Such a contract requires adequate cost and pricing data at specific points in time in the performance of the contract. Another critical situation may develop when a cost-reimbursement or incentive type contract is going to be used. Proper cost accounting systems are extremely important for the seller who anticipates using contract types other than the firm-fixed-price contract. If there is any possibility of a government audit, then adequate cost records and proper accounting systems are mandatory on the part of the seller.

Negotiation

The price and the contract type for a given procurement should never be agreed to by either party during negotiation if there are any other problems or conditions that have not been agreed upon. For example, if the government is going to furnish physical facilities or equipment to the seller, the conditions under which it will be supplied should be clearly spelled out prior to establishing a contract type or price. After all aspects of the procurement have been agreed upon by the negotiating parties, they should then both concur on the contract type that will most likely result in maximum effective performance by the seller.

THE BUYING PROCESS

Any procurement activity undertaken by a government agency or by a firm in industry must by necessity deal with unknown future variables, except for items delivered from current inventory. If the item is taken from inventory, it can be tried and evaluated by the buyer, a reasonable price can be agreed upon, and delivery effected immediately. Under these circumstances, no risk is incurred by either party. However, only a small percentage of items purchased by governments fall into this category.

For nearly all other items, the buying process is different and someone, either the buyer or seller, or in some cases both, must accept the risks of uncertainties with respect to design, production, labor problems, inflation, and delays in delivery. The next section will discuss some important aspects of the buying process as experienced by those marketing products to the government. Because the Federal government is the largest purchaser, the discussion will highlight Federal procurement. However, the same situations can and do exist in procurement activities related to other levels of government.

Complexity of Government Procurement

Buying activities run the gamut from simple to extremely complex. Some small purchases are for standard commercial items which merely involve identifying the item to be purchased and then placing the order at the going market price. However, other purchase activities may be extremely complex. They may involve problems of technology, difficulties in establishing requirements and design for the end product, plus problems of forecasting cost data for a contract that covers several years with the option for additional buys at various times in the future. In many complex purchasing activities, judgments must be made regarding future needs, changes in the economic environment, trends and directions in technology, and the availability and acceptability of cost and pricing data as it pertains to a given procurement action. Generally the most difficult, time consuming, and expensive procurements are those dealing with the purchase of complex systems for the Department of Defense, the National Aeronautical and Space Administration, or the Federal Aviation Administration. Yet many of the same problems, albeit on a smaller scale, are found in procurement actions taken by other federal and state government agencies.

When a government agency places a large contract such as the one for the C-5A aircraft, it affects the total economy of a geographical area. When the prime contract is awarded for a large complex system, the prime contractor must of necessity rely upon subcontractors for doing part of the work. No one firm has the capacity or capability to manufacture a complete plane or complex defense weapon system. Although the prime contract is usually awarded to a large firm in a particular industry, many medium and small size firms are involved as subcontractors. There is competition then for skilled labor, designers, engineers and technicians in the areas where these manufacturing plants are located. This affects the social and economic life of the inhabitants of the areas.

Because large procurements are so complex, the government must constantly be looking for alternative sources of supply so as to maintain some amount of competition among the sellers. In the area of defense, the Defense Department must try to insure that the industries that will be called upon to supply products in time of war maintain and update their technological capability during the peace time. The government then, must work with private industry so that industry's rights with regard to patents and technology are protected, and yet the goals of national defense are always met, i.e., that we get the most up-to-date equipment at the lowest possible cost to the government and the taxpayer.

The Federal government is aware of the impact a large contract has on the economy. In fact, under certain circumstances, policies of the government force the awarding of contracts to firms located in areas of labor surplus. Other Federal policies influence or even dictate the amount of business that must be made available on large contracts to minority and small businesses.

Procuring Complex Systems

The procurement of large complex systems poses many problems for both the buyer and the seller. Figure 5-1 shows the various stages of the procurement of a major system over a period of time. When purchasing any new system in industry, or in the area of national defense, the stages are roughly the same. Using the C-5A aircraft as an example, the first phase consisted of developing the need and concept for the plane. The state of technology had to be considered to determine just what was feasible, while at the same time some initial cost data had to be developed. After the concept was accepted, design and engineering problems had to be overcome. This phase was then followed by a proto type of the plane which in effect tested the engineering and technological capabilities of the manufacturer. After the prototype was accepted and necessary changes were made, limited production could then begin. It was only during these two phases that some reasonable and definite cost data could be generated. Thus having solved most of the unknowns by the final development phase, and having some accurate cost data, it was then possible to write the proper type of contract for the production of the planes.

The process may be terminated at any stage or phase if the buyer determines that the end product will either be unnecessary or will cost too much for the system as a whole. If the process is terminated, the seller is compensated for the work already done. However, the anticipated pay-off, i.e. a large contract, will obviously not materialize. This has happened to many manufacturing companies and it is one of the reasons why the Federal government tries to insure that the firm is reasonably compensated for its efforts. To maintain competition for future projects, the firm may well be needed as a bidder in the future.

TABLE 5-1
Major System Acquisition

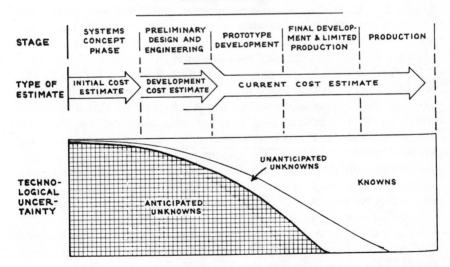

Source: Report of the Commission on Government Procurement, Government Printing Office, Washington, D.C., Dec. 1972, Volume 2, p. 148.

Use of Different Contract Types

Figure 5-1 also indicates why in many procurements, the defense department uses one type of contract for the first stage or two in the acquisition process, and then another type in the latter or final stages when actual production has begun.

During the concept phase and the preliminary design and engineering phase, the contract will normally be a cost-plus-fixed-fee type. There are so many technological unknowns and such limited cost data available, that it is impossible to predict at that point in time how much the final system may cost. For example, in January 1972, the Air Force sent out "requests for proposals" to nine contractors for the initial design and development of an advanced medium short takeoff and landing transport (AMST) aircraft. Five contractors, Boeing, McDonnell Douglas, Bell Aerospace of Buffalo, N.Y., Fairchild Industries of Germantown, Md., and a Lockheed-Georgia/North American Rockwell team responded with bids.

In January 1973, the Air Force announced the award of the contracts to Boeing of Seattle ($95,219,456) and McDonnell Douglas of Long Beach, Calif. ($85,901,510). In phase one of these contracts, the two companies have ninety days to submit additional analyses of possible design/performance trade-offs. The costs for phase one are limited to $2.5 million per contractor.

The Air Force at the end of the ninety days will review the sellers analyses, make its own cost validation studies, and determine whether to initiate the second phase of the contracts. In the second phase, each seller would design, build and test two prototype aircraft using existing engines to be evlauated against project mission requirements. If the prototypes are acceptable, the Air Force may place contracts for production models with only one seller, or it may use both. Generally, however, one design is found superior and the contract goes to the company that designed it.

To further explain this process, in 1972, Fairchild Industries and Northrup had both developed prototype planes for the Air Force for close air support missions. After the Air Force had flown both aircraft for 635.7 hours, the contract was awarded to Fairchild Industries. Fairchild received a cost-plus-incentive-fee contract for $159,279,888 to continue prototype testing and build ten preproduction models for further Air Force testing. The government has an initial option to buy twenty-four to seventy-two production aircraft, which can be exercised after successful testing. This is the new "Fly before you Buy," procurement concept of the Air Force.

In the above case, however, the government also awarded General Electric a fixed-price-incentive contract to develop and deliver thirty-two TF34 engines to power the Fairchild plane. The contract has an option for procurement of sixty-two to one-hundred eighty-six engines for the first production aircraft.

As you can see above, there are two different contract types involved. For Fairchild the technology and cost data are not completely known, so a *cost-plus-incentive* contract is used. However, General Electric has acquired through experience, technical skill and cost data for this type engine, so the contract negotiated is a *fixed-price-incentive* type.

If Fairchild produces more of the planes, then based on firm cost data and technical experienced gained from the initial production runs, a firm-fixed-price-incentive type contract can be used.

Problems of Cost Growth

It becomes apparent that when complex products or systems which require years of lead time for design and development prior to delivery are being procured, many "unknowns" must be considered. It may be necessary to make cost estimates based on insufficient data. Then later when these data are reviewed, often by third parties, it is noted that the cost figures are really too low. Thus in terms of the original estimate, there appears to be a "cost overrun".

The term originally meant "that a contractor's actual expenditures under a cost-reimbursement type contract exceeded the estimated cost initially established in the contract".[1] Usually if the contractor continued work on the contract, the additional cost was paid by the government and the contractor still made the profit originally agreed upon. In the 1960's, several such "cost overruns" were detected and the general public came to believe that the reason was poor estimating, poor management and poor contracting on the part of both buyer and seller. It is true that in many instances, sellers did underestimate cost so as to beat competition and thus "buy-in" to the production stage of the contract. Once they were awarded the prime contract, based on their low cost estimates, it was difficult for the government to get rid of them after major portions of the design and development had been accomplished. This problem has been somewhat overcome by the application of the Truth in Negotiations Act discussed in the next section.

In many instances, costs may well increase even if the negotiators estimate correctly and the contract is properly managed. To take such situations into account, the term "cost-growth" is now used by the procurement agencies.

The most notorious case of cost growth was that of the C-5A in the late 1960's. A more recent episode deals with the increased price of the new B1 bomber. On May 12, 1973, the *Washington Post* stated that the price of the B1 bomber, which is being built by Rockwell International Corp., will increase from a proposed $30 million each in 1970, when the contract was awarded, to approximately $44 million each by 1980. The Air Force explained that the increase is due to design changes and inflation.

Since the C-5A case was brought to light, several studies have been conducted to determine why costs accelerate so much on many of the large complex systems. In 1971, The Department of Defense reported on forty-five systems being procured for a total of $110 billion and found the "cost growth" related to the following: [2]

technical changes account for	20% growth
delivery schedule extensions	17% growth
abnormal economic inflation	18% growth
incorrect estimates	29% growth
other causes	16% growth

Clearly there is no one major reason for cost growth on large contracts. Because of the nature of the reasons, and the unpredictable changes in the economy, cost growth is a phenomena that will continue to plague procurement activities in the future.

Truth in Negotiations Act

The present Truth in Negotiations Act applies primarily to sellers dealing with the Department of Defense, National Aeronautics and Space Administration, and the Coast Guard. However, The Commission on Government Procurement in its recent study recommended that the Act be legally extended to all government procurement agencies. Although the Truth in Negotiations Act has not been written into the Federal Property and Administrative Services Act (the Act that covers most Federal civilian procurement agencies), the content of the Act has been incorporated into the Federal Procurement Regulations and thus does, to some extent, presently apply to civilian agencies subject to the Federal Property and Administrative Services Act.

The present Truth in Negotiations Act requires DoD, NASA, and Coast Guard contractors and subcontractors negotiating contracts of $100,000 or more, to submit to the governments procurement agency, cost or pricing data prior to entering into a negotiated contract. The data must be certified by the seller as being accurate, complete, and current as of the day of agreement by both parties on a price for the contract. If the data are later found to be incorrect, the seller must take a price decrease if the error caused the original price to be too high. At the option of the chief of the procurement agency, certified cost or pricing data must also be supplied by the seller on price changes less than $100,000.

There are three cases when sellers may be exempt from the Act: (1) where price is based on adequate price competition; (2) where price is established by the sale of commercial items sold in substantial quantities to the general public and; (3) where price is set by law or government regulation.

The Act forces the seller to provide cost and pricing data to the government negotiators which puts the government in a better position to determine the validity of the price being negotiated for a particular contract. To the extent that this Act is successful in providing accurate data to the negotiating parties, prices reflecting normal profits for each contract can be agreed upon. This should then help to eliminate excess profits in defense contracts and decrease the need for the use of a re-negotiation board which looks for excess profits after the contract has been completed.

SUMMARY

In nearly all government procurement actions with the exception of small purchases, a contract is used. It is the basic agreement between buyer and seller, and must be executed properly by both parties. If there is a major disagreement during the execution of the contract which cannot be settled by mutual agreement of the parties, the contract may be adjudicated in a court of law.

There are certain basic provisions in Federal contracts that govern the performance of the seller. These provisions are stipulated by law. More specific provisions that reflect the problems of a particular project are written into contracts after lengthy negotiation by both parties. One of the subjects for negotiation is the type of contract to be used. Not all procurements can be made using a fixed-price contract. To allow flexibility in procurement and to give incentive to sellers to cut costs, various types of incentive contracts have been developed. Some are based on the fixed-price contract and some are based on the cost-reimbursement type.

It is important that the contract type utilized matches the procurement action being undertaken. The factors that must be considered when selecting the proper contract type are: (1) the kind of incentive that will best fit the situation and motivate the seller to do the best job; (2) the uncertainties in performance with regard to product design, development and cost data; (3) the environment where the contract will be performed; (4) the accounting system of the seller, and (5) the extent of negotiation that will take place between the buyer and seller.

The buying process as it relates to acquiring modern weapons systems, as well as other complicated systems, is very complex. From the time of conception to the production of the end product, a system goes through many phases dealing with acquisition. Different types of contracts must be used for different phases. During the conception, design, and development phase, a cost-reimbursement incentive type contract is best for handling the vast technological and cost unknowns. As the design becomes firm and prototypes are tested, a fixed-price incentive type contract becomes feasible for the production phase.

Even though the right type of contract is utilized, there is still a problem of "cost growth." However, studies have shown that no one factor is responsible for "cost growth" in a particular contract. Generally such increases in costs can be traced to changes in design and specifications, changes in delivery schedules, incorrect cost estimates, and a high rate of inflation.

One aid now available to government agencies with estimating costs and negotiating prices is the Truth in Negotiations Act. Under certain conditions, this Act requires the contractor (seller) and subcontractor to provide the government with cost or pricing data that is accurate, complete and current when negotiating contracts of $100,000 or more. The results of this Act should be more realistic prices for major contracts, thus eliminating the need for the Renegotiation Board which investigates completed defense contracts for the purpose of recapturing for the government the seller's excess profits.

FOOTNOTES

1. *Report of the Commission on Government Procurement*, Supt. of Documents, Washington, D.C. 1972, Vol. 2, p. 147.

2. *Report of the Commission on Government Procurement*, Washington, D.C., 1972, Vol. I, page 182.

QUESTIONS

1. Why doesn't the government use contracts when making small purchases?

2. Why are there basic general provisions in the standard contracts written by federal procurement agencies? What are the major areas covered by these general provisions?

3. Why are incentives used in various contract types? Who benefits most from the inclusion of such incentives?

4. Why does the government prefer to buy products and services using a fixed-price contract?

5. What are the essential differences between a fixed-price contract and a cost-reimbursement contract?

6. Why does the government prefer not to use the cost-reimbursement contract?

7. Under what conditions would you use a cost-reimbursement incentive contract? Why?

8. What is a letter contract? Why is it considered a "risky" contract to be used by the government?

9. What factors must be considered when determining the proper contract type to use in a procurement action?

10. Why is it adviseable to use more than one contract type in the acquisition of a major weapons system?

11. Explain the reasons for "cost-growth". Do you think these are acceptable reasons? Why or why not?

APPENDIX

STANDARD FORM 32
JUNE 1964 EDITION
GENERAL SERVICES ADMINISTRATION
FED. PROC. REG. (41 CFR) 1-16.101

GENERAL PROVISIONS
(Supply Contract)

1. **Definitions**
   As used throughout this contract, the following terms shall have the meaning set forth below:
   (a) The term "head of the agency" or "Secretary" means the Secretary, the Under Secretary, any Assistant Secretary, or any other head or assistant head of the executive or military department or other Federal agency; and the term "his duly authorized representative" means any person or persons or board (other than the Contracting Officer) authorized to act for the head of the agency or the Secretary.
   (b) The term "Contracting Officer" means the person executing this contract on behalf of the Government, and any other officer or civilian employee who is a properly designated Contracting Officer; and the term includes,

except as otherwise provided in this contract, the authorized representative of a Contracting Officer acting within the limits of his authority.

(c) Except as otherwise provided in this contract, the term "subcontracts" includes purchase orders under this contract.

2. Changes

The Contracting Officer may at any time, by a written order, and without notice to the sureties, make changes, within the general scope of this contract, in any one or more of the following: (i) Drawings, designs, or specifications, where the supplies to be furnished are to be specially manufactured for the Government in accordance therewith; (ii) method of shipment or packing; and (iii) place of delivery. If any such change causes an increase or decrease in the cost of, or the time required for, the performance of any part of the work under this contract, whether changed or not changed by any such order, an equitable adjustment shall be made in the contract price or delivery schedule, or both, and the contract shall be modified in writing accordingly. Any claim by the Contractor for adjustment under this clause must be asserted within 30 days from the date of receipt by the Contractor of the notification of change: *Provided however* that the Contracting Officer, if he decides that the facts justify such action, may receive and act upon any such claim asserted at any time prior to final payment under this contract. Where the cost of property made obsolete or excess as a result of a change is included in the Contractor's claim for adjustment, the Contracting Officer shall have the right to prescribe the manner of disposition of such property. Failure to agree to any adjustment shall be a dispute concerning a question of fact within the meaning of the clause of this contract entitled "Disputes." However, nothing in this clause shall excuse the Contractor from proceeding with the contract as changed.

3. Extras

Except as otherwise provided in this contract, no payment for extras shall be made unless such extras and the price therefore have been authorized in writing by the Contracting Officer.

4. Variation in Quantity

No variation in the quantity of any item called for by this contract will be accepted unless such variation has been caused by conditions of loading, shipping, or packing, or allowances in manufacturing processes, and then only to the extent, if any, specified elsewhere in this contract.

5. Inspection

(a) All supplies (which term throughout this clause includes without limitation raw materials, components, intermediate assemblies and end products) shall be subject to inspection and test by the Government, to the extent practicable at all times and places including the period of manufacture and in any event prior to acceptance.

(b) In case any supplies or lots of supplies are defective in material or workmanship or otherwise not in conformity with the requirements of this contract, the Government shall have the right either to reject them (with or without instructions as to their disposition) or to require their correction. Supplies or lots of supplies which have been rejected or required to be corrected shall be removed or, if permitted or required by the Contracting Officer, corrected in place by and at the expense of the Contractor promptly after notice, and shall not thereafter be tendered for acceptance unless the former rejection or requirement of correction is disclosed. If the Contractor fails promptly to remove such supplies or lots of supplies which are required to be removed, or promptly to replace or correct such supplies or lots of supplies, the Government either (i) may by contract or otherwise replace or correct such supplies and charge to the Contractor the cost occasioned the Government thereby, or (ii) may terminate this contract for default as provided in the clause of this contract entitled "Default." Unless the Contractor corrects or replaces such supplies within the delivery schedule, the Contracting Officer may require the delivery of such supplies at a reduction in price which is equitable under the circumstances. Failure to agree to such reduction of price shall be a dispute concerning a question of fact within the meaning of the clause of this contract entitled "Disputes."

(c) If any inspection or test is made by the Government on the premises of the Contractor or a subcontractor, the Contractor without additional charge shall provide all reasonable facilities and assistance for the safety and convenience of the Government inspectors in the performance of their duties. If Government inspection or test is made at a point other than the premises of the Contractor or a subcontractor, it shall be at the expense of the Government except as otherwise provided in this contract: *Provided*, That in case of rejection the Government shall not be liable for any reduction in value of samples used in connection with such inspection or test. All inspections and tests by the Government shall be performed in such a manner as not to unduly delay the work. The Government reserves the right to charge to the Contractor any additional cost of Government inspection and test when supplies are not ready at the time such inspection and test is requested by the Contractor or when reinspection or retest is necessitated by prior rejection. Acceptance or rejection of the supplies shall be made as promptly as practicable after delivery, except as otherwise provided in this contract; but failure to inspect and accept or reject supplies shall neither relieve the Contractor from responsibility for such supplies as are not in accordance with the contract requirements nor impose liability on the Government therefor.

(d) The inspection and test by the Government of any supplies or lots thereof does not relieve the Contractor from any responsibility regarding defects or other failures to meet the contract requirements which may be discovered prior to acceptance. Except as otherwise provided in this contract, acceptance shall be conclusive except as regards latent defects, fraud, or such gross mistakes as amount to fraud.

(e) The Contractor shall provide and maintain an inspection system acceptable to the Government covering the supplies hereunder. Records of all inspection work by the Contractor shall be kept complete and available to the Government during the performance of this contract and for such longer period as may be specified elsewhere in this contract.

6. Responsibility for Supplies

Except as otherwise provided in this contract, (i) the Contractor shall be responsible for the supplies covered by this contract until they are delivered at the designated delivery point, regardless of the point of inspection; (ii) after delivery to the Government at the designated point and prior to acceptance by the Government or rejection and giving notice thereof by the Government, the Government shall be responsible for the loss or destruction of or damage to the supplies only if such loss, destruction, or damage results from the negligence of officers, agents, or employees of the Government acting within the scope of their employment; and (iii) the Contractor shall bear all risks as to rejected supplies after notice of rejection, except that the Government shall be responsible for the loss, or destruction of, or damage to the supplies only if such loss, destruction or damage results from the gross negligence of officers, agents, or employees of the Government acting within the scope of their employment.

7. Payments

The Contractor shall be paid, upon the submission of proper invoices or vouchers, the prices stipulated herein for supplies delivered and accepted or services rendered and accepted, less deductions, if any, as herein provided. Unless otherwise specified, payment will be made on partial deliveries accepted by the Government when the amount due on such deliveries so warrants; or, when requested by the Contractor, payment for accepted partial deliveries shall be made whenever such payment would equal or exceed either $1,000 or 50 percent of the total amount of this contract.

8. Assignment of Claims

(a) Pursuant to the provisions of the Assignment of Claims Act of 1940, as amended (31 U.S.C. 203, 41 U.S.C. 15), if this contract provides for payments aggregating $1,000 or more, claims for moneys due or to become due the Contractor from the Government under this contract may be assigned to a bank, trust company, or other financing institution, including any Federal lending agency, and may thereafter be further assigned and reassigned to any such institution. Any such assignment or reassignment shall cover all amounts payable under this contract and not already paid, and shall not be made to more than one party, except that any such assignment or reassignment may be made to one party as agent or trustee for two or more parties participating in such financing. Unless otherwise provided in this contract, payments to an assignee of any moneys due or to become due under this contract shall not, to the extent provided in said Act, as amended, be subject to reduction or setoff. (The preceding sentence applies only if this contract is made in time of war or national emergency as defined in said Act and is with the Department of Defense, the General Services Administration, the Atomic Energy Commission, the National Aeronautics and Space Administration, the Federal Aviation Agency, or any other department or agency of the United States designated by the President pursuant to Clause 4 of the proviso of section 1 of the Assignment of Claims Act of 1940, as amended by the Act of May 15, 1951, 65 Stat. 41.)

(b) In no event shall copies of this contract or of any plans, specifications, or other similar documents relating to work under this contract, if marked "Top Secret," "Secret," or "Confidential," be furnished to any assignee of any claim arising under this contract or to any other person not entitled to receive the same. However, a copy of any part or all of this contract so marked may be furnished, or any information contained therein may be disclosed, to such assignee upon the prior written authorization of the Contracting Officer.

9. Additional Bond Security

If any surety upon any bond furnished in conncection with this contract becomes unacceptable to the Government or if any such surety fails to furnish reports as to his financial condition from time to time as requested by the Government, the Contractor shall promptly furnish such additional security as may be required from time to time to protect the interests of the Government and of persons supplying labor or materials in the prosecution of the work contemplated by this contract.

10. Examination of Records

(The following clause is applicable if the amount of this contract exceeds

$2,500 and was entered into by means of negotiation, but is not applicable if this contract was entered into by means of formal advertising.)

(a) The Contractor agrees that the Comptroller General of the United States or any of his duly authorized representatives shall, until the expiration of three years after final payment under this contract, have access to and the right to examine any directly pertinent books, documents, papers, and records of the Contractor involving transactions related to this contract.

(b) The Contractor further agrees to include in all his subcontracts hereunder a provision to the effect that the subcontractor agrees that the Comptroller General of the United States or any of his duly authorized representatives shall, until the expiration of three years after final payment under the subcontract, have access to and the right to examine any directly pertinent books, documents, papers, and records of such subcontractor, involving transactions related to the subcontract. The term "subcontract" as used in this clause excludes (i) purchase orders not exceeding $2,500 and (ii) subcontracts or purchase orders for public utility services at rates established for uniform applicability to the general public.

11. Default

(a) The Government may, subject to the provisions of paragraph (c) below, by written notice of default to the Contractor, terminate the whole or any part of this contract in any one of the following circumstances:

(i) if the contractor fails to make delivery of the supplies or to perform the services within the time specified herein or any extension thereof; or

(ii) if the Contractor fails to perform any of the other provisions of this contract, or so fails to make progress as to endanger performance of this contract in accordance with its terms, and in either of these two circumstances does not cure such failure within a period of 10 days (or such longer period as the Contracting Officer may authorize in writing) after receipt of notice from the Contracting Officer specifying such failure.

(b) In the event the Government terminates this contract in whole or in part as provided in paragraph (a) of this clause, the Government may procure, upon such terms and in such manner as the Contracting Officer may deem appropriate, supplies or services similar to those so terminated, and the Contractor shall be liable to the Government for any excess costs for such similar supplies or services: *Provided,* That the Contractor shall continue the performance of this contract to the extent not terminated under the provisions of this clause.

(c) Except with respect to defaults of subcontractors, the Contractor shall not be liable for any excess costs if the failure to perform the contract arises out of causes beyond the control and without the fault or negligence of the Contractor. Such causes may include, but are not restricted to, acts of God or of the public enemy, acts of the Government in either its sovereign or contractual capacity, fires, floods, epidemics, quarantine restrictions, strikes, freight embargoes, and unusually severe weather; but in every case the failure to perform must be beyond the control and without the fault or negligence of the Contractor. If the failure to perform is caused by the default of a subcontractor, and if such default arises out of causes beyond the control of both the Contractor and subcontractor, and without the fault or negligence of them, the Contractor shall not be liable for any excess costs for failure to perform, unless the supplies or services to be furnished by the subcontractor were obtainable from other sources in sufficient time to permit the Contractor to meet the required delivery schedule.

(d) If this contract is terminated as provided in paragraph (a) of this clause, the Government, in addition to any other rights provided in this clause, may require the Contractor to transfer title and deliver to the Government, in the manner and to the extent directed by the Contracting Officer, (i) any completed supplies, and (ii) such partially completed supplies and materials, parts, tools, dies, jigs, fixtures, plans, drawings, information, and contract rights (hereinafter called "manufacturing materials") as the Contractor has specifically produced or specifically acquired for the performance of such part of this contract as has been terminated; and the Contractor shall, upon direction of the Contracting Officer, protect and preserve property in possession of the Contractor in which the Government has an interest. Payment for completed supplies delivered to and accepted by the Government shall be at the contract price. Payment for manufacturing materials delivered to and accepted by the Government and for the protection and preservation of property shall be in an amount agreed upon by the Contractor and Contracting Officer; failure to agree to such amount shall be a dispute concerning a question of fact within the meaning of the clause of this contract entitled "Disputes." The Government may withhold from amounts otherwise due the Contractor for such completed supplies or manufacturing materials such sum as the Contracting Officer determines to be necessary to protect the Government against loss because of outstanding liens or claims of former lien holders.

(e) If, after notice of termination of this contract under the provisions of this clause, it is determined for any reason that the Contractor was not in default under the provisions of this clause, or that the default was excusable under the provisions of this clause, the rights and obligations of the parties shall, if the contract contains a clause providing for termination for convenience of the Government, be the same as if the notice of termination had been issued pursuant to such clause. If, after notice of termination of this contract under the provisions of this clause, it is determined for any reason that the Contractor was not in default under the provisions of this clause, and if this contract does not contain a clause providing for termination for convenience of the Government, the contract shall be equitably adjusted to compensate for such termination and the contract modified accordingly; failure to agree to any such adjustment shall be a dispute concerning a question of fact within the meaning of the clause of this contract entitled "Disputes."

(f) The rights and remedies of the Government provided in this clause shall not be exclusive and are in addition to any other rights and remedies provided by law or under this contract.

12. Disputes

(a) Except as otherwise provided in this contract, any dispute concerning a question of fact arising under this contract which is not disposed of by agreement shall be decided by the Contracting Officer, who shall reduce his decision to writing and mail or otherwise furnish a copy thereof to the Contractor. The decision of the Contracting Officer shall be final and conclusive unless, within 30 days from the date of receipt of such copy, the Contractor mails or otherwise furnishes to the Contracting Officer a written appeal addressed to the Secretary. The decision of the Secretary or his duly authorized representative for the determination of such appeals shall be final and conclusive unless determined by a court of competent jurisdiction to have been fraudulent, or capricious, or arbitrary, or so grossly erroneous as necessarily to imply bad faith or not supported by substantial evidence. In connection with any appeal proceeding under this clause, the Contractor shall be afforded an opportunity to be heard and to offer evidence in support of its appeal. Pending final decision of a dispute hereunder, the Contractor shall proceed diligently with the performance of the contract and in accordance with the Contracting Officer's decision.

(b) This "Disputes" clause does not preclude consideration of law questions in connection with decisions provided for in paragraph (a) above: *Provided*, That nothing in this contract shall be construed as making final the decision of any administrative official, representative, or board on a question of law.

13. Notice and Assistance Regarding Patent and Copyright Infringement

The provisions of this clause shall be applicable only if the amount of this contract exceeds $10,000.

(a) The Contractor shall report to the Contracting Officer, promptly and in reasonable written detail, each notice or claim of patent or copyright infringement based on the performance of this contract of which the Contractor has knowledge.

(b) In the event of any claim or suit against the Government on account of any alleged patent or copyright infringement arising out of the performance of this contract or out of the use of any supplies furnished ro work or services performed hereunder, the Contractor shall furnish to the Government, when requested by the Contracting Officer, all evidence and information in possession of the Contractor pertaining to such suit or claim. Sucn evidence and information shall be furnished at the expense of the Government except where the Contractor has agreed to indemnify the Government.

14. Buy American Act

(a) In acquiring end products, the Buy American Act (41 U.S. Code 10 a—d) provides that the Government give preference to domestic source end products. For the purpose of this clause:

(i) "Components" means those articles, materials, and supplies, which are directly incorporated in the end products;

(ii) "end products" means those articles, materials, and supplies, which are to be acquired under this contract for public use; and

(iii) a "domestic source end product" means (A) an unmanufactured end product which has been mined or produced in the United States and (B) an end product manufactured in the United States if the cost of the components thereof which are mined, produced, or manufactured in the United States exceeds 50 percent of the cost of all its components. For the purposes of this (a) (iii) (B), components of foreign origin of the same type or kind as the products referred to in (b) (ii) or (iii) of this clause shall be treated as components mined, produced, or manufactured in the United States.

(b) The Contractor agrees that there will be delivered under this contract only domestic source end products except end products:

(i) which are for use outside the United States;

(ii) which the Government determines are not mined, produced, or manufactured in the United States in sufficient and reasonably available commercial quantities and of a satisfactory quality;

(iii) as to which the Secretary determines the domestic preference to be inconsistent with the public interest; or

(iv) as to which the Secretary determines the cost to the Government to be unreasonable.

(The foregoing requirements are administered in accordance with Executive Order No. 10582, dated December 17, 1954.)

15. Convict Labor

In connection with the performance of work under this contract, the Contractor agrees not to employ any person undergoing sentence of imprisonment at hard labor.

16. Contract Work Hours Standards Act—Overtime Compensation

This contract, to the extent that it is of a character specified in the Contract Work Hours Standards Act (40 U.S.C. 327—330), is subject to the following provisions and to all other applicable provisions and exceptions of such Act and the regulations of the Secretary of Labor thereunder.

(a) Overtime requirements. No Contractor or subcontractor contracting for any part of the contract work which may require or involve the employment of laborers or mechanics shall require or permit any laborer or mechanic in any workweek in which he is employed on such work to work in excess of eight hours in any calendar day or in excess of forty hours in such workweek on work subject to the provisions of the Contract Work Hours Standards Act unless such laborer or mechanic receives compensation at a rate not less than one and one-half times his basic rate of pay for all such hours worked in excess of eight hours in any calendar day or in excess of forty hours in such workweek, whichever is the greater number of overtime hours.

(b) Violation; liability for unpaid wages; liquidated damages. In the event of any violation of the provisions of paragraph (a), the Contractor and any subcontractor responsible therefore shall be liable to any affected employee for his unpaid wages. In addition, such Contractor and subcontractor shall be liable to the United States for liquidated damages. Such liquidated damages shall be computed with respect to each individual laborer or mechanic employed in violation of the provisions of paragraph (a) in the sum of $10 for each calendar day on which such employee was required or permitted to be employed on such work in excess of eight hours or in excess of his standard workweek of forty hours without payment of the overtime wages required by paragraph (a).

(c) Withholding for unpaid wages and liquidated damages. The Contracting Officer may withhold from the Government Prime Contractor, from any moneys payable on account of work performed by the Contractor or subcontractor, such sums as may administratively be determined to be necessary to satisfy any liabilities of such Contractor or subcontractor for unpaid wages and liquidated damages as provided in the provisions of paragraph (b).

(d) Subcontracts. The Contractor shall insert paragraphs (a) through (d) of this clause in all subcontracts, and shall require their inclusion in all subcontracts of any tier.

(d) Records. The Contractor shall maintain payroll records containing the information specified in 29 CFR 516.2(a). Such records shall be preserved for three years from the completion of the contract.

17. Walsh-Healey Public Contracts Act

If this contract is for the manufacture or furnishing of materials, supplies, articles, or equipment in an amount which exceeds or may exceed $10,000 and is otherwise subject to the Walsh-Healey Public Contracts Act, as amended (41 U.S. Code 35-45), there are hereby incorporated by reference all representations and stipulations required by said Act and regulations issued thereunder by the Secretary of Labor, such representations and stipulations being subject to all applicable rulings and interpretations of the Secretary of Labor which are now or may hereafter be in effect.

18. Equal Opportunity

(The following clause is applicable unless this contract is exempt under the rules and regulations of the President's Committee on Equal Employment Opportunity (41 CFR, Chapter 60). Exemptions include contracts and subcontracts (i) not exceeding $10,000, (ii) not exceeding $100,000 for standard commercial supplies or raw materials, and (iii) under which work is performed outside the United States and no recruitment of workers within the United States is involved.)

During the performance of this contract, the Contractor agrees as follows:

(a) The Contractor will not discriminate against any employee or applicant for employment because of race, creed, color, or national origin. The Contractor will take affirmative action to ensure that applicants are employed, and that employees are treated during employment, without regard to their race, creed, color, or national origin. Such action shall include, but not be limited to, the following: employment, upgrading, demotion or transfer; recruitment or recruitment advertising; layoff or termination; rates of pay or other forms of compensation; and selection for training, including apprenticeship. The Contractor agrees to post in conspicuous places, available to employees and applicants for employment, notices to be provided by the Contracting Officer setting forth the provisions of this nondiscrimination clause.

(b) The Contractor will, in all solicitations or advertisements for employees placed by or on behalf of the Contractor, state that all qualified applicants will receive consideration for employment without regard to race, creed, color, or national origin.

(c) The Contractor will, in all solicitations or advertisements for employees placed by or on behalf of the Contractor, state that all qualified applicants will receive consideration for employment without regard to race, creed, color, or national origin.

(c) The Contractor will send to each labor union or representative of workers with which he has a collective bargaining agreement or other contract or understanding, a notice, to be provided by the agency Contracting Officer, advising the said labor union or workers' representative of the Contractor's commitments under this nondiscrimination clause, and shall post copies of the notice in conspicuous places available to employees and applicants for employment.

(d) The Contractor will comply with all provisions of Executive Order No. 10925 of March 6, 1961, as amended, and of the rules, regulations, and relevant orders of the President's Committee on Equal Employment Opportunity created thereby.

(e) The Contractor will furnish all information and reports required by Executive Order No. 10925 of March 6, 1961, as amended, and by the rules, regulations, and orders of the said Committee, or pursuant thereto, and will permit access to his books, records, and accounts by the contracting agency and the Committee for purposes of investigation to ascertain compliance with such rules, regulations, and orders.

(f) In the event of the Contractor's noncompliance with the nondiscrimination clause of this contract or with any of the said rules, regulations, or orders, this contract may be canceled, terminated, or suspended in whole or in part and the Contractor may be declared ineligible for further Government contracts in accordance with procedures authorized in Executive Order No. 10925 of March 6, 1961, as amended, and such other sanctions may be imposed and remedies invoked as provided in the said Executive order or by rule, regulation, or order of the President's Committee on Equal Employment Opportunity, or as otherwise provided by law.

(g) The Contractor will include the provisions of paragraphs (a) through (g) in every subcontract or purchase order unless exempted by rules, regulations, or orders of the President's Committee on Equal Employment Opportunity issued pursuant to section 303 of Executive Order No. 10925 of March 6, 1961, as amended, so that such provisions will be binding upon each subcontractor or vendor.* The Contractor will take such action with respect to any subcontract or purchase order as the contracting agency may direct as a means of enforcing such provisions, including sanctions for noncompliance: Provided, however, that in the event the Contractor becomes involved in, or is threatened with, litigation with a subcontractor or vendor as a result of such direction by the contracting agency, the Contractor may request the United States to enter into such litigation to protect the interests of the United States.

Unless otherwise provided, the Equal Opportunity Clause is not required to be inserted in subcontracts below the second tier except for subcontracts involving the performance of 'construction work' at the 'site of construction' (as those terms are defined in the Committee's rules and regulations) in which case the clasue must be inserted in all such subcontracts. Subcontracts may incorporate by reference the Equal Opportunity Clause.

19. Officials Not To Benefit

No member of or delegate to Congress, or resident Commissioner, shall be admitted to any share or part of this contract, or to any benefit that may arise therefrom; but this provision shall not be construed to extend to this contract if made with a corporation for its general benefit.

20. Covenant Against Contingent Fees

The Contractor warrants that no person or selling agency has been employed or retained to solicit or secure this contract upon an agreement or understanding for a commission, percentage, brokerage, or contingent fee, excepting bona fide employees or bona fide established commercial or selling agencies maintained by the Contractor for the purpose of securing business. For breach or violation of this warranty the Government shall have the right to annul this contract without liability or in its discretion to deduct from the contract price or consideration, or otherwise recover, the full amount of such commission, percentage, brokerage, or contingent fee.

21. Utilization of Small Business Concerns

(a) It is the policy of the Government as declared by the Congress that a fair proportion of the purchases and contracts for supplies and services for the Government be placed with small business concerns.

(b) The Contractor agrees to accomplish the maximum amount of subcontracting to small business concerns that the Contractor finds to be consistent with the efficient performance of this contract.

22. Utilization of Concerns in Labor Surplus Areas

(The following clause is applicable if this contract exceeds $5,000.)

It is the policy of the Government to place contracts with concerns which will perform such contracts substantially in areas of persistent or substantial labor surplus where this can be done, consistent with the efficient performance of the contract, at prices no higher than are obtainable elsewhere. The Contractor agrees to use his best efforts to place his subcontracts in accordance with this policy. In complying with the foregoing and with paragraph (b) of the clause of this contract entitled "Utilization of Small Business Concerns," the Contractor in placing his subcontracts shall observe the following order of preference: (I) persistent labor surplus area concerns which are also small business concerns; (II) other persistent labor surplus area concerns; (III) substantial labor surplus area concerns which are also small business concerns; (IV) other substantial labor surplus area concerns; and (V) small business concerns which are not labor surplus area concerns.

POLITICAL INFLUENCE AND MARKET INTEGRITY

One of the major dissimilarities between state and federal buying is the organizational proximity of the chief purchasing official to the chief executive. In some states, the purchasing official reports directly to the governor and in other states, is separated by one organizational position. The governor as an elected official frequently owes favors to certain groups who supported his election campaign and the fear is that favors will be returned through interference in the purchasing function of the state.

This organizational proximity arouses the citizen's suspicion about the objectivity of state purchasing and sometimes this suspicion may be justified. Irregularities in the handling of government affairs by politicians and reported events like the following incident involving Mayor Richard Daley's son in Chicago tend to become generalized in the minds of citizens about the integrity of state and local procurement.

"Daley Son Gets City Business'

"One of Mayor Richard Daley's sons, John Patrick Daley, 25, is an insurance broker for an agency that has sold millions of dollars of insurance on public facilities . . . .

Young Daley joined Heil and Heil, Inc., a North suburban Evanston firm last year. Shortly afterward, there were massive switches of insurance coverage on public facilities to Heil and Heil."[1]

Instances such as these reinforce a prevalent belief that the specter of political influence looms large in state purchasing. This may be true, but valid evidence is rarely obtainable. However, a professionalism movement in states has an increasing number of states' purchasing personnel being selected by merit from civil service rolls rather than by political appointment. In some states, the head of the purchasing department is appointed by the governor. However, the buyers are civil service positions. In eleven states, the head of the purchasing function is selected on the basis of civil service examination.[2]

This trend toward professionalism is important for the development of good government buyer-marketer relationships. A professional approach by purchasing officials will assure that the marketplace remains open to the seller who offers a superior product. Favoritism closes the market to new firms desiring to enter the competition. Since government purchasing is premised on the creation of active competition in bidding, nothing could compromise this more than for competitive firms to suspect that a new contract will probably be awarded to a politically favored marketer.

CENTRALIZED PURCHASING[3]

The intermittent movement of the states towards creation of a central office within the state organizational framework that would be charged with the efficient acquisition and distribution of goods began in the late nineteenth century. Beginning in 1892, Texas authorized the creation of what was to become known as a centralized purchasing function. Other states followed as they experienced many difficulties in meeting their growing needs for goods and services.

Centralized purchasing means the delegation to one office of the authority to purchase supplies, materials, services, and equipment needed for use by the operating branches of the state government.[4] As states realized they were paying retail prices for goods, and in other ways experiencing diseconomies in purchasing, the trend to centralized purchasing accelerated early in the twentieth century.

In a 1967 survey by the Council of State Governments, it was revealed that forty-seven states and Puerto Rico had established a centralized purchasing unit. It is safe to say that in attempting to do business with state government today, a marketer will usually find himself dealing with a state purchasing unit that has well-developed policies and practices, and who tries to help the interested seller become knowledgeable about these policies and practices before he makes a bid on a procurement.

The activities included in the term centralized purchasing are not standardized from state to state. They differ in the extent of goods and services they buy for other state units and what those units can buy for themselves, whether or not purchasing is responsible for a centralized warehouse activity, and how much inter-government purchasing assistance (such as between state and county government or between state and city government) occurs. Therefore, it cannot be stated with certainty what specific goods and services centralized purchasing would be responsible for from state to state. The marketer must investigate and inform himself of each state's purchasing organization that he is interested in doing business with.

Organization for Purchasing

There are many arrangements used by the states in the organizational placement of the purchasing unit. Some have it reporting directly to the governor, others to a financial official, and still others to a managerial type of director. Under the chief purchasing official may be a wide variety of activities such as the procurement of commodities, management of a centralized warehouse activity, handling products made in penal institutions, disposal of surplus or scrap items, and so on. Some states have a specifications group, although frequently this may be a separate office that provides staff support to the buying unit.

Within the purchasing office, organization can take a variety of forms depending on the scope of duties assigned to it by the state. The organization of the Pennsylvania Bureau of Purchases illustrates one type of purchasing organization, although it should not be considered necessarily typical of the majority of states. An abstract of Pennsylvania's organizational structure appears in Figure 6-1.

FIGURE 6-1
Organization For Pennsylvania Procurement

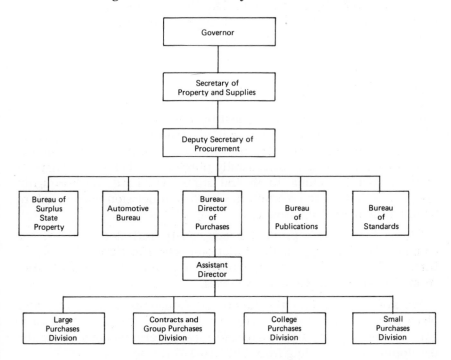

Source: G. R. Brittingham, Jr. (ed.), *How To Do Business With the Commonwealth*, Pennsylvania Bureau of Purchases, Harrisburg, Penn., 1968.

There are interrelationships between the bureaus and divisions, particularly between the Bureau of Standards and the four major divisions. The divisions depend on the Bureau to provide standards and specifications which are the heart of the bidding process. This will be elaborated on in the discussion of the procurement process.

Further specialization occurs within the purchasing office as buyers tend to become specialized in commodities much as they do in industrial purchasing offices. A buyer may be responsible for more than one product or service classification. For example, in Table 6-1, for the State of Maryland Purchasing Bureau, one buyer might have responsibility for department A, two buyers for department B, another for department C, D, and E, another for department F, and finally a sixth buyer for departments G and H. This specialization would primarily reflect both the volume of purchases and the difficulty experienced in buying the various commodities.

The many varieties of purchasing organizational structures found from state to state reflect many factors. Some states have recently embraced centralized purchasing and thus are still reorganizing to find the best structure for themselves. Some state governments want the purchasing function highly placed in government and others want it placed lower organizationally. The location and structure of the purchasing organization is an evolving process with the most ideal arrangement yet to be found by many states.

Scope of Needs

In servicing the needs of the institutions and agencies of the state, a centralized purchasing unit will need every imaginable sort of product. However, each state has different statutory limits on the scope of items that may be centrally purchased. Therefore, a marketer interested in selling to several states will have to thoroughly research each state to ascertain the important decision-makers before building the marketing program.

The scope of state product needs can be reflected in either the commodities bought, or the functional classifications of expenditures. Table 6-1 illustrates the range of commodities which varies from vegetable seeds to motor vehicles.

We saw in Chapter I the functional categories into which states place their money. Table 6-2 further illustrates the functional category of spending for both state and local governments by listing the development of spending from 1966 to 1971.

TABLE 6-1
Specialization Within the Purchasing Office: State of Maryland

Department A

AA	Anthracite Coal	AB	Bituminous Coal

Department B

BA	Stationery	BH	Farm & Road Machinery & Supplies
BB	Musical Instruments		(Including Stable Supplies)
BC	Arms & Ammunition	BI	Broom Shop Supplies
BD	Laboratory Apparatus & Supplies	BJ	School Supplies & Classroom Furniture
BE	Field Seeds	BK	Books & Periodicals
BF	Vegetable Seeds	BL	Signs, License Tags & Badges
BG	Flower Seeds, Bulbs & Greenhouse Supplies	BN	Dairy Supplies
		BO	Live Stock

Department C

CA	Drugs & Pharmaceuticals	CE	Paints, Oils & Glass
CB	Petroleum Products	CG	Tobacco, Pipes, Etc.
CC	Building & Road Materials	CJ	Chemicals, Heavy Industrial
CD	Lumber & Millwork	CK	Chemicals, Laboratory Chemicals & Biochemicals

Department D

DA	Orchard Supplies	DG	Hospital Equipment & Sundries
DB	Nursery Stock, Ornamental Plants & Shrubbery	DH	Holiday Goods
		DI	Bakery Products
DC	Fertilizer	DJ	Groceries
DD	Meats, Dairy Products & Poultry	DK	Frozen Foods
DE	Flour	DL	Fresh Fruits & Vegetables
DF	Live Stock Feed	DM	Seafood, Fresh & Frozen

Department E

EB	Paper, Twine & Paper Articles	EE	Office Business Machinery
EC	Office Furniture	EH	Janitor Supplies & Sanitary Chemicals

Department F

FA	House Furnishings	FI	Dental Supplies
FB	Tin Cans	FJ	Athletic Goods
FD	Footwear	FK	Laundry Supplies & Equipment
FE	Household Furniture	FL	Photo & X-Ray Supplies
FF	Clothing	FM	Beauty Shop Supplies & Equipment
FG	Notions	FP	Mattresses & Pillows
FH	Dry Goods	FR	Leather & Shoe Findings

Department G

GA	Heat, Power Plant & Plumbing Supplies	GH	Civil Engineering & Drafting Materials
GB	Tools	GI	Refrigeration & Air Conditioning
GC	Carpenter & Hardware Supplies	GJ	Iron, Steel & Ornamental Iron Work
GE	Tinship Supplies	GL	Motor Vehicles
GF	Electrical Supplies	GM	Motor Vehicle Accessories & Supp.

Department H

HA	Printing	HD	Printing & Duplicating Equipment & Supplies

Source: Courtesy of Mr. Stanley J. Hanna, Chief of the Purchasing Bureau, Baltimore, Maryland, October, 1971.

TABLE 6-2
Trend of State and Local Spending of Selected
Functional Categories: 1966-1971

Functional Category	Amount (millions of dollars)				
	1970-71	1969-70	1968-69	1967-68	1966-67
Total	170 766	148 052	131 600	116 234	105 978
General Expenditure	150 674	131 332	116 728	102 411	93 350
Education	59 413	52 718	47 238	41 158	37 919
Local Schools	41 766	37 461	33 752	29 305	27 590
Institutions of Higher Educ. .	14 785	12 924	11 551	10 214	8 932
Other Education	2 861	2 332	1 935	1 637	1 397
Highways	18 095	16 427	15 417	14 481	13 932
Public Welfare	18 226	14 679	12 110	9 857	8 218
Hospitals	9 086	7 863	7 011	6 282	5 559
Health	2 119	1 806	1 509	1 264	1 081
Police Protection	5 228	4 494	3 901	3 410	3 049
Local Fire Protection	2 303	2 024	1 793	1 623	1 499
Sewerage	2 646	2 167	1 895	1 732	1 635
Sanitation Other than Sewerage	1 411	1 246	1 074	975	888
Local Parks and Recreation ...	2 109	1 888	1 645	1 412	1 291
Natural Resources	3 082	2 732	2 552	2 471	2 344
Housing and Urban Renewal ..	2 554	2 138	1 902	1 632	1 469
Airports	1 061	969	723	516	466
Water Transport and Terminals	504	444	461	407	319
Parking Facilities	159	158	137	105	144
Correction	1 885	1 626	1 391	1 270	1 139
Libraries	761	700	634	573	518
Employment Security Administration	945	769	667	606	547
Financial Administration	2 271	2 030	1 806	1 610	1 468
General Control	3 027	2 652	2 299	2 037	1 845
General Public Buildings	1 405	1 287	1 209	1 037	931
Interest on General Debt	5 089	4 374	3 732	3 266	3 032
Other and Unallocable	7 276	6 140	5 622	4 686	4 057
Utility Expenditure	8 675	7 820	7 316	6 721	6 006

Source: *Government Finances in 1970-71*, U.S. Department of Commerce, Bureau of the Census, October 1972, GF 71, No. 5, pp. 18-19.

In general, total spending has increased at a fairly even rate over the five years. However, this reflects inflationary value of the dollar and increased wages for employees as well as enlarged need for goods and services. While state government has tried to stabilize its expenditures, city government has found it necessary in recent years to spend more for police protection, water and sewage capability, and local schools to meet population requirements.

State Agency Buying Autonomy

Many states have found that centralized purchasing offers no advantages for some of their needs. For this reason, the state statutes may exempt certain of its agencies, such as the department of highways or educational institutions, from centralized buying and allow them to do their own buying. Similarly, certain commodities such as perishable foods may be exempted and be purchased at the point of use.[6]

The exemptions by agency or commodity from centralized purchasing vary greatly by state and largely reflect the population needs of the state and in some cases, the recency with which the state has adopted centralized purchasing. The Council of State Governments surveyed the states in 1967 on their practices and Table 6-3 illustrates their findings on state agency buying autonomy. California, Colorado, and New Hampshire are states that allow relatively little agency autonomy. Arkansas, Ohio, and Iowa are examples of states that allow relatively greater agency buying authority.

Higher education institutions and authorities are most likely to have independent buying power limited only by a spending ceiling or an amount of money above which further power must be requested from the state comptroller or legislature. The "authority" listed at the top of the columns refers to a municipal business corporation set up by the state to administer some important function such as a major toll bridge, toll-road, or port such as the New York Port Authority. Frequently these authorities administer some transportation activity for the state as an independent buying unit.

The commodities which are exempted from central purchasing are generally consistent with the state agencies that are given their own buying power. Table 6-4 illustrates the commodities by states which are *not* purchased centrally. Textbooks, professional services, utility services, and election materials are common examples of these.

Some states have created problems for marketers by making the buying exemption of an agency *optional* to the preference of the agency. The option may apply to some items, all items, or be changeable depending on the particular purchase contemplated. The inconsistencies this encourages, and the resultant confusion among marketers about where the decision authority resides in a purchase, is an undesirable consequence. This not only discourages doing business with the state, but may also result in poor buyer-seller relationships due to government buck-passing and evasiveness in buying decisions.

Inter-Governmental Purchasing Cooperation

Almost one-half of the states have statutes which create the opportunity for city and county governments to obtain assistance from the state centralized purchasing unit. This inter-government cooperation may extend to participating in a state purchase, drawing goods from a state stores warehouse, or obtaining assistance in

TABLE 6-3
State Agencies Which Buy Commodities and Services Independently of the Central Purchasing Agency
(Excluding construction contracts)

State	Universities	Senior Colleges	Junior Colleges	Community colleges	Technical institutes	Highway departments	Elective offices	Supreme court	Lower courts	Legislature	State fair	Authorities (port, etc.)	Explanatory notes
Alabama	×	×		×	×						×	×	
Alaska	×			×							×	×	
Arizona		(a)	×	×									
Arkansas	×		×	×	×	×	×	×	×	×			(a) Some colleges buy independently.
California	×									×			
Colorado							×		×	×			
Connecticut							×	×	×	(b)			(b) Central purchasing acts in advisory capacity only.
Delaware (1)	(c)	(c)	(c)	×	×	(c)	(c)	×	×	×	×	×	(c) Central purchasing handles certain items only.
Florida	(c)	(c)		×	×	(c)		×		×	×	×	
Georgia				×			×	×	×	×	×	×	
Hawaii	×	×	×	×	×		×	×		×	×	×	
Idaho	×	×	×	×	×		×	(d)	×	×	×	×	(d) Central purchasing handles certain items only.
Illinois	×	×	×	×	×		(d)	(d)	(d)	×	×		
Indiana	×				×			×	×		×	×	
Iowa	×	×	×	×	×	×	×		×	×		×	
Kansas			×		×				×				No agencies purchase independently.
Kentucky				×		×							
Louisiana	×	×	×		×						×	×	
Maine	×	×	×	×	×							×	(e) Optional with agency.
Maryland	(e)						×			×	×	(e)	(f) Agencies buy some items independently.
Massachusetts	(f)	(f)	(f)							×	×	×	

Montana
Nebraska (i)
Nevada
New Hampshire (j)
New Jersey
New Mexico
New York (k)
North Carolina
North Dakota
Ohio (l)
Oklahoma
Oregon (n)
Pennsylvania
Rhode Island
South Carolina
South Dakota (o)
Tennessee
Texas
Utah
Vermont
Virginia (p)
Washington (q)
West Virginia (r)
Wisconsin
Wyoming

(i) These buy some items independently.
(j) Rutgers University buys independently.
Information not available.
(k) Optional with agency.
No agencies purchase independently.
(l) Optional with agency.
(m) Governor's Office, State Treasurer buy independently.
(n) Except where state funds involved
(o) Agencies buy some items independently.
Water districts buy independently.
(p) Central purchasing handles certain items.
(q) Agencies buy some items independently.
(r) Central purchasing controls procedures.
Game & Fish Commission buys independently.

State Purchasing for Political Sub-Divisions

SOURCE: The Council of State Governments, *Purchasing among the States*, 1967 and Jennings, op. cit., pp. 98-99. Reprinted by permission. (1) Does not have central purchasing. (2) Central purchasing function is limited.

specifications to be used in purchasing. Little is known about the extent of this cooperation or the frequency of state help to city and government purchasing.

In the 1967 survey of the states, it was revealed that most states allow local government purchasing units a "permissive" or optional status on whether state purchasing help is sought. Table 6-5 shows that only two states, North Carolina and Texas, have statute provisions which make it mandatory that political subdivisions buy certain goods through the state unit.

The benefits and drawbacks of this cooperation in purchasing depend on the viewpoint taken. From the political subdivision viewpoint, the practice is good because better specifications permit greater control in buying, and participating in larger purchases obtains the lowest possible price from marketers.

From the state purchasing office and the marketer's viewpoint it may have disadvantages. Here again, as in the case of optional agency buying, to the extent that political sub-divisions tend to come in and go out of state purchasing programs, confusion is added to the orderly handling of contracts in the buyer's office. On the other hand, marketers may be unsure of when they should have liaison with the state office. The state office may have difficulty handling the city or town portion of the purchase order because there are different purchasing policies used by the various governments. These problems can be alleviated if the political subdivisions regularly participate in central purchasing programs and only adjust the quantity they want. Then all parties can adjust to the situation and know how to handle themselves most effectively.

THE BUYING PROCEDURE

The buying process begins when a need originates someplace in the state and results in a written requisition forwarded to the central purchasing office. Even in a state small in land area or population, 50,000 or more of these requisitions will be processed in a year. To handle this volume, a systematic procedure is needed.

The buying procedure should be regarded as "given" to the marketer seeking a contract with the state in that it cannot be modified by his efforts. Therefore, it is something that must be researched and understood precisely before attempting to obtain orders.

For the purpose of an overview, the procedure can be reduced to the following steps. A need arises and after the availability of funds is checked, a requisition is forwarded to the purchasing office. Specifications are then determined, bids or negotiations are conducted, and a purchase contract is created. When delivery is made, the items are inspected and certified that they meet conditions of the contract and if they do, the invoice is checked and payment is made. For the marketer, the steps leading to the award of the contract or purchase order are the most critical. Finding or generating the need, conforming to the specifications, and successful bidding involve good market liaison and can be viewed as the key elements in a market program that exploits government markets. Continued liaison and performance to contract conditions are the elements of maintaining the market program.

Requisitions and Specifications

A need arises many ways. An equipment marketer can contact a hospital and persuade the technicians and administrator that they need his testing instrument, but until a written request for its purchase is initiated in the form of a requisition, it remains a need. At regular intervals, the state warehouse will initiate a requisition to replenish inventory levels. The governor can initiate legislation to authorize the construction of a building for administrative use. Regardless of the source, the buying process begins with a recognized legitimate need and the generation of a request to buy.

State purchasing, like households, must live within its means. By law, a certain amount of money is allotted by the legislature each year for major categories of purchase and before purchasing can progress any further, a check must be made to assure that all available funds for the fiscal year are not used up. Before a marketer tries to convince an agency to buy his product, it would be prudent to inquire into the fiscal availability of funds. The time may not be right for persuasion.

The origin of the need somewhere in the state organization, the development of a requisition, and the checking of available funds before purchasing has a parallel with the procedure used in larger industrial firms. The only major difference thus far is that in a firm, if a buyer must exceed budgeted limits, an executive decision is needed. In the state, an emergency appropriation by the legislature would be required and this is seldom done.

At this point, a detailed description of the product, a *specification*, is needed. If the item needed has previously been purchased, then a valid specification may exist. If the item has not been purchased for a long time or has never been purchased, then the purchasing may turn to the ultimate user and a state technical support unit, such as the Bureau of Standards in Pennsylvania, to create the specification.

The specification document is very important to both the buyer and the marketer. For the buyer, it becomes the standard against

TABLE 6-4
Classes of Commodities and Services Not Purchased Through The Central Purchasing Agency

State	Textbooks	Library books and periodicals	Perishable foods	Liquor	Medical and dental supplies	Professional services	EDP installations	Printing	Election materials	Insurance	Highway construction equipment	Highway construction materials	Technical instruments or equipment	Livestock	Water, light, etc.
Alabama	X			X					X	X				X	X
Alaska				X			X			X				X	X
Arizona	X	X		X			X	X	X					X	X
Arkansas	X	X		X			X	X	X	X					X
California			X		X	X			X		X	X	X		X
Colorado	X			X							X				
Connecticut						X	X			X					
Delaware*															
Florida	X	X	X	X	X	X	X		X			X	X		
Georgia				X		X			X						
Hawaii	X	X		X			X	X	X	X		X	X	X	X
Idaho			X	X			X		X						X
Illinois			X	X		X	X		X						X
Indiana				X		X			X						X
Iowa				X		X			X						X
Kansas				X		X	X	X	X	X				X	
Kentucky	X			X		X			X	X	X			X	X
Louisiana	X	X		X		X					X	X			
Maine	X	X	X	X		X		X		X					X
Maryland	X	X		X		X	X		X	X	X	X			X
Massachusetts	X		X			X	X			X		X		X	X
Michigan				X		X									X
Minnesota						Some		X	X						X
Mississippi*								X	X						X

State													
Montana	x				x	x	x	x			x		x x x
Nebraska	x	x	x		x	x	x	x					x
Nevada	x	x	x		x	x	x	x	Some				x
New Hampshire	x		x		x	x		x				Some	x
New Jersey	x		x		x		x	x					
New Mexico (a)	x				x			x					
New York	x	Some	x	Some	x	x	x	x					x
North Carolina	x	x	x	x	x	x	x	x		Some		x	x
North Dakota	x	Some	x	x	x	x	x	x	x			x	x
Ohio	x		x		x		x	x		x			x
Oklahoma	x		x	x	x	x	x	x					x
Oregon	x		x	x x		x	x	x					x
Pennsylvania	x	x	x	x	x	x	x	x				x	x
Rhode Island	x		x				x x	x					
South Carolina	x	x	x x	x	x	x	x	x		Some		x	x
South Dakota	x	x	x	Some	x	x	x	x	x		Some	x	Some
Tennessee			x				x						x
Texas	x	x	x	x	x	x	x	x					x x
Utah			x	x			x x						
Vermont			x	x			x						
Virginia	x		x		x		x		x	x		x	x
Washington	x	x	x	x		x	x x	x	Some	Some		x	
West Virginia							x	x					
Wisconsin							x		x				x
Wyoming			x		x								x

SOURCE: The Council of State Governments, *Purchasing among the States*, 1967 and Jennings, op. cit., pp. 100-101.   Reprinted by permission.

* Delaware and Mississippi do not have central purchasing on a broad base.

(a) Information not available.

which the marketer's product performance will be measured. The marketer would like the specification to be slanted as much as possible towards his product so that he has a competitive edge over other bidders. At the very least, he must be fully knowledgeable about the specifications so that he doesn't have to perform uncompensated development work to modify his product so that it conforms to the specification. The specification is made fully available to bidders before they compete for the contract or order.

The specification that supports the bidding process can involve a spot or one-time purchase such as a computer or bridge, or it can be used for an extended period of time as in a *term contract*. The latter is a contracted purchase that covers multiple orders over a time period, usually twelve months. During the year, many orders for delivery can be placed routinely since the specification covers the life of the contract. Changes in the specification can only be made with the concurrence of both buyer and seller.

Bidding or Negotiation

Once the details of the needed product are determined, the buyer begins to contact marketers in order to establish the price and other terms of sale. Two principle methods are used; either bidding or negotiation. When the product need can be adequately specified in advance, bidding is the preferred method. However, there are many occasions when the need is not adequately specified, as well as many other situations, when negotiation is the better method of arriving at a transaction. In both methods, the objective is to create as much active competition as possible and therefore the lowest price to the state.

Bidding can be either formal or informal. Many states have statutes requiring advertising of the bids when the order exceeds a specified amount of money. This means that the purchasing office must advertise the purchase in newspapers, mail notice to known suppliers, and in other ways disseminate information so that as many marketers can compete for the purchase as is practicable. However, all states make the distinction between this *formal* invitation to bid and a *solicitation of prices* in the form of quotations. The latter is a more informal means of making purchases for minor expenditures, proprietary articles, or repair parts. Since marketers are primarily interested in larger purchases, more needs to be explained about formal bidding.

The state buyer maintains lists of qualified marketers for all commodities. These firms are mailed an invitation to bid which consists of all of the information needed to submit a formal sealed bid. It is good strategy for the marketer interested in doing business

TABLE 6-5
State Purchasing for Political Subdivisions

State	For cities, counties, towns	For school districts	For quasi state agencies	Premissive	Mandatory	Statutory
Alabama	On request	On request	On request	X		X
Alaska	No	No	No			
Arizona	No	No	No			
Arkansas	No	No	No			
California	Yes	Yes	Yes	X		X
Colorado	No	No	No			
Connecticut	No	No	Yes	X		X
Delaware (a)						
Florida	Yes	Yes	Yes	X		X
Georgia	No	No	No			
Hawaii	No	No	No			
Idaho	No	No	No			
Illinois	Rarely	No	Rarely	X		X
Indiana	No	No	No			
Iowa	No	No	No			
Kansas	No	No	Yes	X		
Kentucky	No	No	No			
Louisiana	Yes	Yes	Yes	X		X
Maine	Yes	Yes	No	X		X
Maryland	No	No	No			
Massachusetts	No	No	No			
Michigan	Yes	No	Yes	X		X
Minnesota	Yes	Yes	Yes	X		X
Mississippi (b)						
Missouri	No	No	No			
Montana	No	No	No			
Nebraska	No	No	No			
Nevada	Yes	Yes	Yes	X		X
New Hampshire	Yes	Yes	No	X		
New Jersey	No	No	Yes	X		X
New Mexico (b)						
New York	Yes	Yes	No	X		X
North Carolina	No	Yes	No		X	X
North Dakota	Yes	Yes	Yes	X		
Ohio	No	No	No			
Oklahoma	Yes	No	No	X		X
Oregon	Yes	No	Yes	X		X
Pennsylvania	No	No	No			
Rhode Island	No	No	No			
South Carolina	Yes	Yes	Yes	X		X
South Dakota	No	No	Yes			
Tennessee	No	No	No			
Texas	No	Some items	No		X	X
Utah	On request			X		X
Vermont	No	No	Yes	X		
Virginia	Yes	No	Yes	X		X
Washington	No	No	No			
West Virginia	Rarely	Rarely	Rarely	X		X
Wisconsin	Yes	Yes	Yes	X		
Wyoming	No	No	No			

Source: The Council of State Governments, National Association of State Purchasing Officials, *Purchasing among the states.* (Chicago: National Association of State Purchasing Officials, 1967) and Jennings, op. cit., p. 61. Reprinted by permission.

(a) Does not have central purchasing.
(b) Information not available.

with state purchasing to contact the state office and have the firm certified as a qualified vendor *before* the bidding process begins.

At an appointed place, date, and time, the bids are opened public- ly. It is required by law that any interested person may attend the bid opening and hear the individual bids read aloud. The bid informa- tion is then placed in a record which must be kept available for inspection for two years. If a firm consistently fails to bid, an inquiry will be made into the reasons why. If the reason is judged to be unsatisfactory, that marketer will be dropped from further bid invita- tions.

Once the bid is tabulated and the lowest price among the qualified marketers is determined, the award is made. A purchase order is prepared and signed by both buyer and seller. Once delivery is made, the goods are inspected for compliance with specifications and payment is then made.

When purchasing products such as typewriters, paper, fertilizer, and blankets, formal bidding is the favored procedure. But in purchasing the repair of a bridge, Polaroid Land cameras, or an electron microscope, more flexibility in purchasing procedure is needed and the *negotiation* process provides it.

Negotiation simply means that the purchasing official will discuss and bargain the state's needs with several potential suppliers and, within the constraints he faces in terms of time and money, try to obtain the best purchase he can. The specification, price, delivery schedule, payment schedule, certification of performance procedure, and many other matters may all be subjects of the discussion. The most common situations leading to negotiated procurement include:

— When the dollar value of the order falls below a minimum level.
— When there is reasonable evidence that bidders have colluded in formal bidding.
— When the purchase involves a proprietary item available from only one source.
— When obtaining repair parts or other items peculiar to special- ized equipment.
— When the state has an emergency need and the items must be available in a short time period.
— When a contract is being renewed.[7]

From the state's point of view, negotiation is considered an alternative procedure to the preferred mode of operation, formal bidding. Therefore, even though the marketer strives to differentiate his product in order to free him from some of the pressures of competition, he can expect reluctance from buyers to use the nego- tiation process.

Many state purchasing statutes have a provision that may require marketers on both bidding and negotiation to place both a bid and performance bond. Presumably, the bid bond is an assurance of good faith, and the performance bond helps to assure performance per contract. The bid bond may be waived, if it is not required by law, when the purchasing official knows that the firm has performed satisfactorily in the past. The performance bond is used extensively and is not as likely to be waived.

PROBLEMS IN THE MARKET PROCESS

There are always problems in realizing industrial or consumer markets and state government marketing is no exception. Imperfections creep in and make the buying-selling process less effective than it could be. Some problems are primarily those faced by buyers and others by sellers, although many of the problems have some effect on both buyer and seller.

While the evidence on the magnitude of the problems does not exist, studies by the Council of State Governments and conversations with the chief purchasing official in several states confirms that there are problems which both buyer and seller must be prepared to handle. The following problems should be considered illustrative rather than exhaustive.

From the Buyer's Viewpoint

Four problems experienced by state buyers stand out as directly affecting the purchasing process. These involve the necessity to improve buyer capabilities, the exemptions from state purchasing which creates inconsistencies, buyer collusion, and inadequate manpower in the buying office.

The enlarging scope of centralized purchasing responsibilities in many states has caught some of the offices with buyers who have less than the necessary background to handle their job effectively. There is a recognized need to upgrade the qualifications of those people who would become state buyers so that they will have the sophistication that has already been developed in the sales engineers who are sent by marketers to call on them. There is also a need for regular training programs to upgrade the buyers knowledge about state policies, and buying practices, as well as new product technologies in the commodities that the buyers are responsible for. These changes will assist the states in obtaining better purchasing as well as helping those marketers that really do have an improved product to offer the state to attract the interest of buyers.

The second problem centers around the exemptions from central purchasing that many states give to certain state agencies and the exemption of certain commodities. In some cases, the exemptions make sense. The hospital or school has needs unique to its functions and since it is the only user, it can most effectively deal with marketers. The same is true for certain commodities, particularly perishable foods or nuclear materials. However, in some states, the statutes give the autonomous agency the option to participate in state purchasing contracts and this creates the same problem experienced in political subdivision purchasing cooperation. To the extent the autonomous agencies come in and go out of the contracts, confusion and inconsistencies result in the handling of the contract resulting in dissatisfaction for all parties. The simplest remedy is to routinize the cooperation so that over time, everyone knows what to anticipate when a purchase is to be made.

Occasionally, a group of bidders collude against the state by offering very similar prices and offerings. A well known example of this was the 1961 electrical goods cases involving some of the largest manufacturers in the United States.[8] Purchasing officials suspect that collusion happens much more than is detected. Collusion can involve price fixing or market allocation and either one has the effect of diminishing competition for bids. This, in turn, may raise the price that states pay for goods. Through close surveillance of bids, the strategy available to buyers is to use the negotiation process if collusion is suspected.

The final buyer problem is an organizational one. Many state purchasing offices find they lack enough manpower and other resources to properly do all that is expected of them. Feeling the pressure to supply the state functional agencies in a reasonable time period leads to rushed buyers and taking short-cuts in the buying process. This is undesirable in that it loosens purchase control and may raise the price paid for products. Tired, hurried buyers may make mistakes and this may cause headaches for marketers.

From the Marketer's Viewpoint

The problems that marketers must contend with include getting added to bidders' lists, the preference given to in-state marketers, favoritism that results when political influence is applied for a firm, and occasionally, the geographical spread of using agencies in the state. Political influence and the bidders' list problems are the most serious problems.

In the bidding procedure, state purchasing wants effective competition among bidders to result in the lowest price to the state. However, there are limits to the number of competitors that the purchasing office can deal with. Therefore, the problem is that the state office often has more requests to be included on the bidders' list than can be effectively accommodated. Some marketers will be left out but the question is — who? Vendor analysis is important in this situation. By using criteria stressing financial reliability, quality of product, experience, and general reliability, the lists can be reduced so that new firms may be added. Some offices lack the time to regularly up-date their lists and where this happens, the new marketer may have difficulty getting placed on the bidder's list and receiving an invitation to bid.

The state's citizens are not particularly interested in subsidizing state firms and where the state has statutory provisions giving preference to in-state marketers, subsidizing may result. Local marketers already have an advantage in transportation costs over out-of-state marketers anyway. By putting out-of-state marketers at a further disadvantage, competition is compromised and prices paid for goods may be higher than they should be.

The constitutionality of in-state preference has been questioned[9] and the National Association of State Purchasing Officials has come out strongly against the practice.[10] However, the practice continues and restrains the market opportunity available to out-of-state marketers.

The third problem relates to political interference with the purchasing process in favor of one particular marketer. This unfairly diminishes the opportunity of other marketers and may result in poorer quality products and higher prices for the state.

Most purchasing officials resist political pressure and handle their responsibility with professional integrity. However, the potential for the problem cannot be dismissed. The governor may wish to return favors to business supporters, and a state legislator may have a specific interest in having a marketer in his election district favored in the award of contracts. An appointed purchasing official is much more likely to respond to these pressures than is a career civil service official. The only way a marketer can become forewarned about this problem is to inquire about the firm that was previously awarded the contract and study the bid records.

The final problem is one frequently experienced by industrial marketers. It is often necessary to personally contact the users of the product as well as the buyers. In large states with geographically spread-out users, the costs of personal selling and maintenance efforts greatly increase the price that must be charged for the goods. For example, assume a marketer of office duplicating equipment wins a state contract. The machines will be used in dozens of locations around the state. The marketer's personnel must travel thousands of miles training the ultimate users in how to use the machines, making repairs, and performing normal maintenance. Since all marketers face the same problem, it seldom poses a unique disadvantage for one marketer. However, the marketer must be a good forecaster of machine breakdowns and treat repairs separately in his bid. Maintenance programs may be priced separately anyway.

SUMMARY

Each of the fifty states annually purchases quantities of a myriad of products and services. This represents huge market opportunity for many manufacturers and wholesalers as well as an important caveat: know the buying environment of each state before seeking opportunities to bid on contracts. While most of states have a centralized buying office which facilitates transactions, the states are far from uniform in their procurement statutes, policies, procedures, and attitudes toward marketers. In a strict sense, each commodity sold in each state should be treated as a separate market to be researched and monitored.

Many states allow purchase exemptions from centralized buying. Agencies such as a university or hospital may be allowed to purchase for their own needs. In addition, certain commodities are unique and therefore purchased at the point of use. A penal institution would purchase its own meats and fresh produce because of its perishable nature while other needs may be purchased by the state office. Therefore a marketer may have to be prepared to find and maintain contact with several locations in the state if he is to win and maintain government contracts. Optional buying opportunities for agencies to participate in state purchases introduces complications into contracts and are considered a problem by both the state buying office and some marketers.

The buying process used by a state has a definite sequence and marketers must understand it thoroughly to be effective. It begins with a need being expressed by a form, the requisition to buy. Availability of funds is checked by the buying office and then a product specification is matched to the requisition. The bidding or negotiation process is then begun to attract marketers with the lowest price. They are contacted from a bidder's list which is a file of all qualified, responsive firms who are known to be able to supply the state's needs.

This part of the process is strategically the most important to sellers. One strategy is to develop the need by persuading state agencies to want a product or service and thereby get a requisition generated. A second strategy is to influence the product specification so that it favors one competitor's version of the product over others. An even more vital strategy is to get the firm's name placed on the bidder's list so it will have an opportunity to participate. Once the contract has been won, the sensible strategy is to perform exactly as the product specification and contract stipulates, and to maintain constant liaison with the buyer to keep him informed of progress.

The process is concluded when the products are delivered and inspected for contract conformance. Maintenance of machinery is usually covered under a separate contract and would therefore not delay payment of the first contract.

This simplified representation of the buying process does not reveal the numerous problems associated with accomplishing the steps. Some of the more important complications which hinder the effective working were presented from the buyers and sellers viewpoints. From the buyers side of the market, the problems included were the lack of adequate manpower, the need for more training of the buyers to update their expertise, and the complications which arise when sellers collude to set price or in other ways to divide the market between them.

The sellers side of the market sees other problems. Principal among their difficulties are the preference some states give to instate marketers on contract awards, political interference which applies favoritism in awards to politically favored firms, and occasionally, the trouble some firms have in getting placed on the bidder's list. These problems serve to close market opportunity for firms and discourage participation in state government markets.

Many states are working to overcome these defects because the ultimate effect of all of these is to raise the price as the quality of goods they buy is lowered. One positive trend in this direction is the selection of buyers and officers by civil service procedures rather than being appointed by the governor. This lessens political pressure and political patronage in the decisions on contract awards.

FOOTNOTES

1. "Dailey Son Gets City Business" *Washington Post*, February 9, 1973, Section A, page 3.

2. George W. Aljian, Ed., *Purchasing Handbook*, 2nd Edition, McGraw-Hill Book Co., 1966, Section 19, p. 14.

3. This chapter depends greatly on the study by George W. Jennings, *State Purchasing*, published by The Council of State Governments, Lexington, Kentucky, 1969.

4. Russell Forbes, *Centralized Purchasing*, rev. ed., National Association of Purchasing Agents, New York, 1941, p. 5.

5. *How To Do Business With the Commonwealth*, Bureau of Purchases, Commonwealth of Pennsylvania, June 1968. Most states offer a brochure similar to this to aid marketers in orienting to the central purchasing office.

6. Aljian, op. cit., Section 19, page 7.

7. Jennings, op. cit., page 88.

8. "The Incredible Electrical Conspiracy", *Fortune*, Part I in April, 1961, pp. 132-7, and Part II in May, 1961, pp. 161-4.

9. *Washington Law Review*, Vol. 40, (April, 1965), pp. 49-67.

10. *In-State Preference in Public Purchasing*, Council of State Governments. Chicago, July, 1965.

QUESTIONS

1. What does "centralized purchasing" mean when applied to states? What advantages does it offer to both buyer and seller?

2. The trend of total state expenditures for goods and services has risen steadily upward in the last five years. What underlying causes account for this?

3. Interview buyers in the buying office of your university and examine the extent of buying autonomy given the university by the state. What are the limits to the autonomy and what is the

rationale for them? Take the viewpoint of a buyer and then a seller and discuss whether the limits should be increased or decreased.

4. Draw a flow-chart of the buying process sequence in state government centralized purchasing. In a strategic sense, which steps are most important to a marketer? Why?

5. Why is the product specification a key element in the buying process?

6. Explain the activities involved in formal bidding or advertised bids. What role does the bidder's list play in this? What can a firm do if it is not on the bidder's list when the bidding begins?

7. What do buyers maintain are the problems with the buying process? What needs to be done to remedy these problems?

8. What do sellers maintain are the problems with the buying process. What needs to be done to remedy the problems?

MARKETER STRATEGY: 7
PREPARING TO SELL

The first six chapters have primarily dealt with description and analysis of the buyer's side of government markets in order to understand the requirements and environment that affect the buying process. This chapter and the next change orientation to the seller's side of the market. The objective is to elaborate on some of the more important procedures and strategies that enable sellers to find and participate in government market opportunities.

ORIENTATION TO MARKETS

In order to begin at the beginning, let's assume that the marketing firm is wondering whether or not to enter government markets. It is unfamiliar with all aspects of governmental purchasing and before it is willing to commit any resources, the Vice-President of Marketing wants to have a good understanding of the opportunities available and the risks they involve.

All of the marketing principles that apply to consumer or industrial markets apply to government markets. In fact, it is frequently more critical to apply them well since the markets are dynamic and the buyer is exacting.

Thoroughly researching the market in terms of customer needs, buying procedures, trends of change, competitors, and the buying environment is the first critical principle. Whereas approximate measures of these may allow a marketer to make a profit in commercial markets, in government markets it may well result in a large financial loss on contracts. The prospective marketer will quickly learn that his customer expects him to be objective, factual, exact, prompt, and if he is a manufacturer, to demonstrate that he has managerial, engineering, and production expertise.

The environment controlling government markets is constantly changing. Legislatures modify existing needs, change procurement policies, and add new needs. A dynamic market is one that must constantly be kept in touch with. Any firm wanting to do business with governments has a second principle to deal with: It will have to be organized for a continual liaison with the influencers, deciders, buyers, and users that affect the purchase of his product.

A third principle relates to organization. Exploiting markets requires excellent research and careful planning to set out courses of action which will make the sales profitable. An important part of the planning is establishing an effective internal organization which can attract contracts and enable the firm to perform adequately on them. Except where standardized, "off-the-shelf" items are being sold, the firm may find it necessary to establish a new type of internal organization to handle government contracts. Instead of a sales-manager, a contract administrator knowledgeable about government procedures and policies is often needed. Instead of salesmen, engineers with good communication skills may be the only people who can influence the sophisticated government personnel that surround the buying process, particularly in federal research and development contract and major systems work.

Many firms have found it necessary to establish an organization that parallels the organization of the buyer. This is common in industrial marketing as well. The underlying reason is sound: *People communicate best with those of similar backgrounds.* In large federal systems purchases will be found engineers, contracting officers, auditors, lawyers, negotiators, inspectors, buyers, logistics officers, and price analysts. The manufacturer's sales team will parallel this with his own engineers, project officer, auditors, price analysts, quality control group, and lawyers. The government person will often prefer to talk with his counterpart in the firm rather than a salesman or executive. Controlling this communication parallelism is vital so that all levels of the firm's organization are kept informed of changes that affect contracts.

Knowing the precise need of the customer, being thoroughly familiar with how he purchases and uses the product, creating a mechanism that allows the seller to know of changes affecting the market, and developing an organization in the firm that can success-fully perform market requirements are all examples of established marketing principles which are especially applicable to governmental marketing. These examples serve to illustrate their importance but constitute only the beginning of a successful approach to these markets. Once the marketing manager accepts the idea that a govern-ment buyer is as exacting as the most precise buyer he has ever dealt with, he has the proper orientation to make preparation for these selling opportunities.

To Sell or Not?

A more fundamental question for the firm to consider than "how to sell" is "whether or not to sell" to government markets. In earlier chapters, it has been suggested that there are both reasons for and against entering this area of marketing. A review of these would now be appropriate.

Some motivations for seeking government contracts include the utilization of excess production capacity, utilization of an engineering or research capability more fully, thereby making a contribution to overhead, a gain in research support for technology which could be transferred to commercial market products, and of course, an increase in total sales. Singly, or in combination, they form a compelling argument for seeking government orders.

Offsetting these objectives are some market requirements that may prove hard to adjust to, as well as involving some risks. Governments will make every effort to squeeze what they believe to be excess profit out of a contract. On the other hand, they may insist that the firm fully meet the contractual agreement even though it may mean a large financial loss to the firm. Cost figures will be carefully scrutinized and have to be justified in bidding. In some cases, company records may have to be opened to the view of government auditors. Quality control procedures are often dictated and a formidable set of documentation papers will be required to certify compliance with all contract clauses. Finally, governments chose to enforce social legislation through their purchasing contracts which often causes unforeseen costs to the firm. Examples of these include the hiring of minority personnel, giving subcontracting preference to small business firms, and paying the minimum wage.

When the manager places the cost of these market requirements against his reasons for seeking government business he comes to a significant decision; either he is out of the market or he goes after it. If he does go after it, it is to be a long-run relationship as opposed to a one-sale effort since the costs of organizing for the business can best be retrieved over many contracts. Trade-offs will usually have to be made and the decision is all the more difficult because the real cost of some of the market requirements are difficult to measure.

The Need for Objectives

When seeking government contracts, it is wise to have company and marketing objectives determined. This will have a great deal to do with what contracts are sought, how to price bids, and in general, which company capabilities the firm is desirous of utilizing.

The least applicable objective is to seek a high profit return from investment. This is unlikely to happen. Although much attention has been given to the "military-industrial complex" and "excess profits" in the media, the fact is that many studies have proven that firms achieve an average or below-average profit return on their equity in government contracts. By using competitive bidding, examining company records of procedures and their costs, and using the power to retrieve any profit considered to be in excess of a normal return in development work, governments forestall or retrieve any excess profits.

ESTABLISHING RELATIONSHIPS WITH STATE GOVERNMENT MARKETS

Depending on the commodity, any manufacturer or wholesaler can seek and obtain orders from state governments. It is true that some states do give preference to in-state firms; however, this is actively being discouraged by several groups and states, as discussed in chapter 6. Many times, buyers prefer to deal directly with manufacturers since the lowest price can be obtained, or because the product must be modified in the production process to meet the unique needs of the state. However, there are hundreds of standardized products used by both commercial and government markets in small quantities which allows wholesalers to have a competitive advantage over manufacturers.

Finding and participating in state purchases can be viewed as a three-step process; measuring demand, becoming informed of the buying environment and performing those activities necessary to have the firm added to the bidder's list for the commodity. Little can be generalized about pricing of bids and performance on contracts. Therefore, these will not be discussed. How a firm prices its bids depends largely on the firm's objectives, the competitors it faces, and the costing procedure required by the state purchasing office. Performance on a contract must be exactly to the product specification and clauses in the contract or the firm will face financial penalties plus the loss of future opportunities to bid.

Measuring Demand

It will be recalled that state purchasing procedure is usually initiated by a requisition from an agency, a restocking requisition by warehouse stores, or a reorder by the purchasing office itself. The specification is then either reviewed or developed, budget authority checked, and bids solicited. Since demand can originate from a combination of origins, the marketer should completely orient himself to the origin of the requisition and the buying procedure. For simplicity's sake, measuring demand will be discussed in terms of whether the product has been purchased previously or not.

The activities necessary to determine whether the state needs the products of a firm and the annual usage rate depends on its purchase history. If the state has previously purchased the product and it is centrally purchased, the first step is to visit the state's purchasing office and talk with the particular buyer for that commodity. He will probably know the past usage as well as the projected need for the next year or two. The next step would be to speak personally with the user and requisitioner in the agency. For example, if a wholesaler of office supplies wanted to get a sharper estimate of his market opportunity, he should visit office managers, secretaries, and store supplies people in state buildings, school systems, the state police agency, and other direct-use points. Armed with this information, the wholesaler then knows how he can better serve these points than competitors and therefore how to be more effective in his bidding strategy.

The procedure varies if the firm discovers that the state has never bought the product or service. After checking the budget possibility and other constraints of the state to purchase the product, the firm's representative will have to estimate demand by trying to persuade the user-agency and gauging their interest. This would be true for a manufacturer of a new type of road surfacing machine. In the department of highways, the general supervisor, foremen, and operators would receive information about the machine, and be invited to a demonstration of its performance. At a later time, the firm's engineers could review the specifications for the engineers of the department. Demand stimulation and demand measurement therefore become part of the same effort.

In both the cases of standard and new products, it is wise to estimate demand by visiting the buyer's office as well as the user-agency locations. The buyer knows purchase history, budget authority, and legislated procurement regulations, while the user-agency is most knowledgeable about future needs and problems encountered in using the product.

Some state agencies buy for their own needs instead of going through a central purchasing office and some commodities are purchased at the point of use even though other agency needs are purchased by the central purchasing office. In both cases, the same activities to measure demand are involved, including visiting the agency buyers and users, requesting permission to see the product specification, gathering information on future usage, and finding how the user's needs can be served better than they currently are.

Know the Rules and Competitors

The marketer who has never sold to state markets needs information on procurement procedures and potential competitors. The first strategy would be to become thoroughly familiar with the buyer environment by obtaining copies of the product specification, state regulations on purchasing, a copy of purchasing contracts used by buyers, and information on the organization, procedures, and policies of the purchasing office. Some of these items are available at the state capital building and in some cases, all of these items can be obtained from the buying office. Most states desire to do business with responsible and responsive suppliers and therefore provide all of the materials necessary for the prospective seller to fully orient to their needs and procedures. With some investigation into the state legislative record, the full budget for procurement as passed by the legislature can be found and studied.

Determining who the competitors are, what they sell to the state, how much, and at what price is the next step. Bids on contracts are placed in a public record which is available to any interested party for two years after contract award. By requesting and studying these records, a reasonably accurate assessment of competitors and their offerings can be made. In commercial marketing, this information is difficult or impossible to obtain.

Gaining Placement on the Bidder's List

Having concluded that the firm wishes to pursue state government sales, the next strategy is to have the firm's name added to the list of qualified suppliers.

This can be as easy as simply filling out the appropriate form. However, if the product is technologically sophisticated, then it might be necessary for state personnel to also visit the firm's location to assure that it has the capability to perform adequately on a contract. With less involved products, evidence can be brought to the purchasing office to demonstrate competence in the form of samples, test results, catalogs, and evidence of satisfactory sales to other states.

Getting on the bidder's list may be difficult if the buyer feels that he has enough capable suppliers. Patience and persistence may be the requisite strategy if this is the case. There is turnover on most lists to make room for a new competitor who proves he has a product or service differentiation which translates into a benefit to the state. The differentiating factor may be a superior quality control record, produce-use capabilities, excellent post-purchase servicing, faster delivery on products or spare parts, or many other aspects other than lower price.

Staying on the bidder's list is another matter. Firms are dropped from the list if they fail to respond to request for bids, if collusion in bidding is evident, if bids are poorly prepared, or if they fail to perform satisfactorily on past contracts. The caveat is obvious: keep in constant touch with the buyer and user, personally explain why a bid is not made, and be certain the firm can properly perform any contracts won in terms of the product specification and contract.

ESTABLISHING RELATIONSHIPS WITH
FEDERAL GOVERNMENT MARKETS

The firm thinking of seeking federal government contracts should realize three things right away: First, federal purchasing is surrounded by an entirely different market environment from commercial marketing and this will require the firm to have someone or a group of individuals who must be educated to seek and maintain contact with federal agencies; second, that this liaison will have to be continual because of changes and the numerous influencers, buyers, users, and evaluators who are involved with purchases; and finally, that he is entering a buyer's market where the buyer has a high level of expertise to support him and who expects exact compliance with procedures and contract stipulations. As with commercial marketing, a high level of commitment in resources from the firm may be necessary in order to find and successfully participate in demand opportunities.

Many questions must be answered before a firm is willing to commit the resources needed to sell to the federal government. What is the level of present and future market potential for the product or service? Who are the specific deciders and buyers? What are the obvious and subtle costs associated with sales? What changes will this business require in the way the firm conducts its affairs? How does a firm compete for the business and who are the probable competitors? These and other questions must be answered by an intensive market analysis of federal markets.

Fortunately, in thoroughly investigating these questions, the firm has gone a long way toward preparing itself to bid and perhaps win a federal agency contract.

One way of organizing the firm's strategy for the participation in federal markets is to divide the effort into five phases:

— Orienting to Federal Markets
— Analysing Market Potential
— Participating; Bidding or Negotiation
— Contract Performance Strategies
— Post-Contract Strategies

The first two phases deal with preparing to sell and are discussed in this chapter. Chapter 8 will deal with the three remaining areas of strategies that relate to participation in the markets.

Orienting to Federal Markets

The first task is to gather adequate information about Federal procurement procedures, and the need for products and services, and to study these fully. The person given this responsibility may need a support team of legal, engineering, financial, and production personnel who can advise him on the implications of statements in the documents he will gather.

The search begins by carefully considering the present and desired future capabilities of the firm. What objectives is the firm trying to achieve in utilizing these capabilities by seeking federal contracts? These objectives will be sharpened as information is obtained about various sub-markets. They are necessary if a commitment decision is to be reached and a wise decision is to be made on whether or not to bid on a contract. A frequent objective is to develop the research capability in a certain area that has transfer application to commercial markets or that has long run potential market worth. For example, this might lead a firm to seek a National Aircraft and Space Administration (NASA) contract. The food developed for the astronauts may have limited initial dollar sales volume from the government but the publicity of the moon flights might generate a commercial market for the product such as in the case of the Tang orange beverage concentrate.

OBTAINING SOURCE MATERIALS

The library of materials to be studied will quickly grow. A beginning can be made by obtaining basic reference works which include a detailed description of government contract procedures.[1] Materials may be obtained from the National Contract Management Association, as well as support materials provided by numerous consultants and organizations who annually hold conferences with the general theme "Doing Business with Federal Agencies."

Federal markets are unique when compared to commercial markets in that an overt effort is made by the buyer to facilitate the efforts of their potential suppliers. Inquiries to agencies about opportunities to sell to them will be met with brochures, advice, and sometimes seminars that explain what products the agency buys, how to go about participating, and what will be expected of the seller. The firm's representative should visit the local office of the agency first and then if desired, a telephone call to the Washington, D.C. office may be in order. Initially, a buyer or public information person will be reached. From him the names of the appropriate contract administrator, planners, project engineers and executives associated with a particular product or project can be obtained for interviewing at a later time.

There are several important documents to be obtained from the Superintendent of Documents. The basic procurement regulations to be obtained and carefully studied are the Armed Services Procurement Regulations (ASPR) which governs military and space purchases, and the Federal Procurement Regulations (FPR) which governs civilian purchases.[2] Copies of the President's budget may also be obtained for the past several years to determine the trend of expenditures for projects that involve products that could be offered by the firm.

Through the Superintendent of Documents a subscription can be entered for the *Commerce Business Daily*. This indispensible publication is published daily, Monday through Friday, and contains a wealth of federal market analysis information. Its contents include information on past purchases and the firm that was awarded the contract, new needs for which bids are being sought, announcements concerning government and sponsored seminars, and notices about changes in procedures. Read on a daily basis for a length of time, the CBD quickly becomes a major marketing intelligence source about Federal markets.

Other materials that may be added to the library include trade association literature and trade magazine subscriptions. A survey by the Chamber of Commerce found that ninety-two percent of the business and trade associations were engaged in some type of government relations activities.[3] These include providing information on government needs, legislative activity relating to changes affecting procurement procedures, and advice on trends in these matters. If the firm is interested in the defense department sub-markets, subscription to several of the military oriented trade magazines is desirable. Frequently these contain articles that detail problems in selling systems and sub-systems to those markets as well as current industry opinion on evolving needs in the planning for America's defense posture. Examples of these publications include *Armed Forces Management*, *Aviation Week*, and *The Naval Institute Proceedings*.

INTERVIEWING PEOPLE

The printed information will go a long way toward orientation to federal markets and their buying environment, but is not adequate by itself. The next strategy would be to talk personally with a number of different types of people to get a current, deeper understanding for both the selling opportunity in the foreseeable future as well as the nuances and potential problems of government business.

A visit to the nearest office in the state for a particular agency is appropriate. It may be necessary to go to the Washington office for more detailed information; however, this is not always true. For example, the Department of Defense has many purchasing points around the country that buys research or products. A telephone call to the Pentagon procurement office can find exactly the place in the country to go and visit.

Several types of information may be gained from interviews with buyers and contract administrators. For example, it may be possible to view the product specification on past contracts relevant to what the firm could offer, gain information on future contracts, and obtain the forms required to be added to the bidder's list. If access can be gained to the record of past contract awards, a wealth of additional information is obtained including:

- The specific projects purchased or bid on in the last two years and the product specifications involved.
- The name of the firms who became prime suppliers and who are potential competitors.
- The names of the firms who lost, why they lost, and who are competitors on these contracts also.
- Clues to what it will cost to develop a bid. In some cases, this can cost thousands of dollars.

These and other vital bits of information on contract activity and competitors will greatly aid in the decision on whether or not to seek government contracts and if the firm elects to, the number and strengths of the probable competitors.

Contact with the purchasing offices and study of the *Commerce Business Daily* provides information on business firms who already participate in government contracts. However, a personal visit to the contract administrators of firms in related industries that do business with the federal government will provide insights into government markets from the *sellers* viewpoint. Questions can be asked about their organization for these markets, the impact government sales has had on their internal operations and product lines, and the implications that the multiple types of contracts that government agencies use has for bidding strategy. After interviewing a number of firms, a better understanding of the requirements for an effective marketing program can be determined.

USING WASHINGTON CONSULTANTS

Many firms new to government selling elect to retain a Washington consultant. His contacts and knowledge of government procedures may be invaluable, at least until the firm's sales volume is large enough to sustain the cost of the firm's own full-time personnel there. These consultants are frequently found by recommendation of firms who are active in government markets.

Entry into the government market is free but not necessarily simple. The Federal government buys out of a myriad of offices and has many agencies that monitor the purchasing process. Forms must be filled out, clearances obtained, contract limitations checked, and communications with government clarified. The use of a consultant is basically two decisions: Should one be used to measure market demand and constraints and if the firm elects to seek government contracts, should he be retained to assist in the implementation of the marketing program?

The first question dealing with the measurement of market potential and market constraints will depend greatly on the level of sales desired and the type of product the government needs. If the firm intends to develop a minor fraction of its sales from government markets and is dealing in standardized products, perhaps it can get along without the consultant. If the firm is interested in major systems purchases such as those of NASA, the Atomic Energy Commission, or the Department of Defense, it would be wise to retain a consultant to gather information from numerous Congressional and agency sources. Most consultants specialize by product areas such as radar, computer, naval armaments, etc. which reflects the fact that many of them are former military or engineering people connected with a military service or agency. They tend to further specialize in an area of government (Atomic Energy, Navy, Commerce, Air Force) for the same reason. This specialization allows for a high level of expertise in gathering both engineering and purchasing types of information. Knowledge of the exact location of the information shortens the market intelligence effort time.

After the marketer gains enough experience to have a good understanding of the nature of government markets, learns their peculiarities, and is able to create a mechanism that maintains continual market intelligence in his field of interest, he may no longer need a consultant. The firm will want to establish its own representative near Washington. One of the more compelling reasons for this continual presence derives from the nature of the bidding process. Many contracts when announced leave only a short time period in which to submit a bid, often thirty days. Thirty days is often insufficient time in which to both generate a good proposal on research and development work and make a bid, and therefore, more advance notice is needed. By having a Washington representative visit the funding agency, it is possible to learn of the research or product need sooner and thereby gain additional time to develop the firm's proposal.

People unfamiliar with governmental marketing tend to confuse market consultants with the lobbying efforts of trade and business associations. Consultant persuasion is generally reserved for providing a market liaison for his client. Thus he is concerned with gaining intelligence on the attitudes of Congressional senators or representatives concerning bills that might affect his client, talking with engineering and contract administrators who work on projects, and relaying information from his client to buyers, cost analysts, lawyers, and other government personnel. In short, he performs the sales contact function expected of sales engineers in industrial marketing, but on a broader scale.

Analyzing Market Potential

Having gathered enough information to intelligently assess the federal government market opportunities, the next step is to organize the market information to decide whether or not to enter this area of marketing. If the firm's decision is to seek these sales, then the next step will be to put the firm in a position to bid on contracts.

Reducing the information to a market analyzation format can be best illustrated by an example. Assume that the firm is a medium-sized manufacturer who currently sells metal machined products to industrial firms. The firms assets include precision metal-working machinery and a group of experienced engineers. After gathering source materials and talking with numerous people knowledgeable about government demand, the manager might develop a matrix similar to that illustrated in Figure 7-1. The information search has found that the most probable immediate selling opportunities include the Government Services Administration for his present products, and a U.S. Air Force contract for new, specialized metal parts. The purchases for the military will usually be part of a project or larger systems procurement; therefore a good understanding of the prime contract stipulations is important.

FIGURE 7-1
A Hypothetical Market Analysis for a Manufacturer

Factors	1. Government Services Admin. (GSA) Sub-markets		2. Air Force Sub-markets	
	Federal Supply Service	Transportation Service (motor equipment)	Air Force Systems Command	Air Force Logistics Command
1. *Relating to Customer*				
Product Class/System				
Past Annual Volume				
Initial order				
Space, parts & inventory				
Probable Range/unit				
Purchase Location				
Purchase Contacts				
Buyer				
Project Manager				
Engineer				
Contract Administrator				
Requirements				
Clearance required				
Cost Development Spec.				
Bidding form used				
Timing of bids				
Contract type used for bidding				

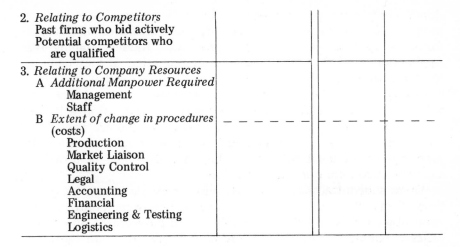

2. *Relating to Competitors* Past firms who bid actively Potential competitors who are qualified				

3. *Relating to Company Resources*
  A *Additional Manpower Required*
    Management
    Staff
  B *Extent of change in procedures*
    (costs)
    Production
    Market Liaison
    Quality Control
    Legal
    Accounting
    Financial
    Engineering & Testing
    Logistics				

Figure 7-1 is only one of many possible matrix analyses that could be designed to facilitate decision making. Organization of the gathered information should center on customer needs and the procurement environment, competitors, and factors influencing the firm. Examples of the latter include the need for additional equipment and manpower, their costs, and modification of procedures that might be required in order to handle government business. In other words, it is necessary to not only measure market potential, but also the meaning that this business would have for the firm if it is sought.

Preparing to do Business

In light of manufacturer's objectives associated with government markets and the knowledge he has of them, he can make the go — no go decision. If he decides to go ahead, there are then several actions he must take.

The first is to assure that he has the organizational capacity to handle the volume of sales he is willing to submit bids for. It is not always necessary to *actually possess* all the money, machines, and manpower, but rather to be able to demonstrate to the satisfaction of the government engineering executives, contract administrators, and buyers *that the firm could quickly assemble these productive factors* and perform satisfactorily if a contract was awarded to the firm. This is a critical step in preparing to solicit government contracts or sub-contracts from prime contractors because the buyer-decision makers must be convinced of this capability to perform. The government doesn't want just low bidders — it wants responsible bidders and "responsible" translates into *capable*.

Armed with evidence of its capability, the firm's representative should contact the procurement offices. In the case of standardized products, the contact can be made by mail. Evidence of past performance can be sent and the appropriate "Bidders Mailing List Application" and clearance forms can be requested. It may be more advisable to personally visit the office to both explain the firm's capability and to be exposed to buyer's viewpoints and frame of reference. Copies of the product or research specification will have already been obtained, so it would be wise to inquire about any impending changes in it. This bidder's list effort should be made with every purchasing location, at both the main office and field offices, to insure maximum opportunity to bid.

Where subcontracts are involved, visits may also be necessary to those firms who have or are likely to have the prime contract. The same objectives apply that were relevant to government purchasing offices: exhibit interest in the business and demonstrate the capability to do the required performance.

Having put the firm in a position to participate in government markets further strategies come into play. In Chapter 8, strategies relating to bidding, performance on contracts, and the post-contract period are discussed.

SUMMARY

This chapter and the next are oriented to recommendations about how marketers can exploit government markets. Just as they are consumer or industrial markets, several basic marketing principles apply: the need to study and thoroughly orient to market needs and environment, to create an internal organization capable of communicating with and responding to market requirements, and to maintain a continual market intelligence capability to be abreast of changes in the market so that the firm can adapt.

A firm contemplating entering government markets faces two key questions: Should I sell to these markets or not? and, What goals am I trying to achieve? Objectives are necessary to guide the firm's search for the best market opportunities. As the search progresses, the firm's researcher will become aware of the unique demands that governments make of firms willing to do business with them. These demands translate into subtle costs which may make the difference between doing business or not. Government markets are not noted for returning large profits on investments.

State government markets represent opportunities for wholesalers and manufacturers but seldom for retailers. Since most states have a centralized buying office, contacting buyers and investigating selling opportunities is easy relative to most federal markets. It may be that a certain commodity is purchased at the point of use in the state, or that a state agency is allowed to procure its own needs. Measuring demand must then be done at those locations. In any case, the location of use should be visited as well as the buying office to learn of future needs and improvements that a marketer can offer to differentiate himself from his competitors in bidding for contracts.

After measuring potential demand, the firm should become thoroughly familiar with the state's procurement regulations, contracts used, buying procedures, product specification, and the probable competitors. All of this information can usually be obtained from the buying office upon request.

Finally, by demonstrating adequate capability to perform, the marketer may have his name added to the bidder's list. This will entitle him to be invited to the bidding when the next purchase is to be made. If the bidder's list is currently filled, the marketer has two strategies open to him: either wait until the buying office drops a competing firm from the list for noncompliance, or demonstrate to the buying office that the firm offers a product clearly superior to the one being used.

Entering Federal markets usually requires much more effort than state markets but the steps are essentially the same: estimate potential of all possible markets, fully orient to the buyers need and his environment, and gain placement on the bidder's list. The marketer may wish to hire a knowledgeable Washington consultant who can perform these steps much quicker than the firm because his stock-in-trade is knowing who and where to contact.

If a consultant is not used, there are many information sources which can be used to inform the potential marketer. The buying offices for agencies, the *Commerce Business Daily*, and numerous periodicals put out by all Federal agencies have the general goal of assisting firms to sell to them. Seminars, other firms that currently do business with agencies, and industry associations can also provide useful information about market potential and the market environment.

Organizing the information in order to weigh the benefits against the costs is the next step. It sometimes happens that the risks of these markets out-weigh the potential benefits of Federal contracts and the firm is wise to drop the idea. If the firm does progress further, the next step is to contact all of the buying offices of the agency that offer contracts the firm is interested in and begin the process of becoming added to the bidder's list.

When the firm is invited to bid on contracts, new strategies come into play. Chapter 8 discusses bidding, contract, and post-contract strategies.

FOOTNOTES

1. Examples of these include W. H. Reiner, *Handbook of Government Contract Administration*, Englewood Cliffs, N.J.: Prentice-Hall, Inc., 1968; G. W. Aljian (Ed.) *Purchasing Handbook*, New York: McGraw-Hill Book Co., 1968; and D. W. Pace, *Negotiation and Management of Defense Contracts*, New York: Wiley-Interscience, 1970.

2. While ASPR and FPR are the basic documents, many Federal agencies have semi-autonomous procurement regulations which must be studied as well. For example, NASA uses NASA PR which is much like FPR except for certain provisions and is published separately.

3. "Survey of Association Activities and Business Problems," U.S. Chamber of Commerce, Washington, D.C., 1961.

QUESTIONS

1. In what ways are government markets dynamic? For each dynamic aspect, what general implications would this have for sellers to government?

2. Name several marketing management principles presented in earlier marketing courses. Does each one apply to government markets; Explain how it does.

3. Why do firms in government markets frequently find it necessary to build a marketing organization that parallels the organization of the government agency being sold to?

4. What function do marketing objectives perform in becoming oriented to the markets?

5. If a state government has never purchased a particular product, what strategies are necessary in order to measure market demand?

6. What information can be gained from the state centralized buying office to prepare a marketer to participate in state contracts?

7. Visit the purchasing office of your school or university and study their purchasing environment. What are the limits of their buying authority? What requirements do they make of sellers who want to participate in purchases? What deficiencies do the buyers note in sellers and their strategies?

8. What can a marketer do if the state buying office tells him that he has all the qualified sellers he needs and therefore will not add the marketer to the bidder's list?

9. State some of the specific information sources that can inform a marketer about federal market potential and the buying environment.

10. Discuss the advantages and disadvantages of using a Washington consultant for finding and participating in Federal contracts.

Once the marketer has decided to consider entering the government markets, he must be prepared to market his products and service in a different way. He must learn about the bidding process and negotiation as a means of establishing a price for his product or services. He must be aware of the possibility of having his completed contract renegotiated, resulting in the government retrieving some of the profits. He must be prepared to adjust his marketing techniques to the peculiarities of this market. These problem areas are the topics of discussion in this chapter.

PRICING BY BIDDING

Bidding is a competitive process for establishing a price for a marketer to contract to produce a product or service. The buyer is interested in paying the lowest price for the product or service. He is usually assured this by accepting the lowest competitive bid provided the bids represent independent assessment of the situation by each firm, i.e., no collusion on the part of firms submitting bids.

To be assured of quality, performance, and delivery, the buyer stipulates these items in the contract. In case a seller is awarded the contract but fails to live up to the terms of the contract, he may be prosecuted and forced to pay damages to the buyer.

Bidding is used in industrial marketing by original equipment manufacturers who request bids on contracts to supply such things as tires for vehicles, spark plugs for engines, and other component parts needed in the manufacture of an end product. A firm that is building an automated mill or production facility may ask machinery and equipment sellers for bids on all or part of the needed equipment. Many industrial construction jobs, such as large dams with power generators, are awarded to the lowest bidder. Janitorial services for buildings are often purchased on the basis of sealed competitive bids. Thus, the bidding process as a pricing method has wide commercial application and is not restricted to government markets.

Bidding on contracts raises some very difficult problems for a seller. He must usually bid on a contract requiring performance in the future, unless the product is in his inventory, which is rarely the case. Thus, various unknowns have to be estimated, such as future labor costs, material costs, and the rate of inflation. The seller never gets the opportunity to revise his bid after it has been submitted. If his bid is accepted and he has forecast costs too low, then he will have to accept the loss on the contract. On the other hand, if his bid is accepted and he can reduce his costs substantially below his estimates, he can under most contracts pocket the extra profits. However, under certain conditions, the Federal government may retrieve any profits it considers excessive. This will be discussed later in the chapter.

Competitive Bidding Strategies

The seller is interested in submitting a bid that will be accepted and at the same time meet his objectives for bidding. If he is primarily interested in profit, then he must bid as high above his costs as possible and still have the bid accepted. In this situation, he would like to bid just under the lowest bidder and have a cost structure low enough to allow a substantial profit margin. How successful he is will be determined to a large extent by the objectives and bids of the competing firms. If the other bidders are not too interested in the contract, the chances are good that they will submit rather high bids. But how does a particular seller know this before he submits his bid? This is really the core of the bidding problem and requires some experience and judgment on the part of each potential seller.

The objectives of each seller with regard to the potential contract will influence the bids they submit. For example, if a firm needs work to keep its production force together in the short-run, it may submit a very low bid based on its marginal cost or even below it, in order to insure winning the contract. The firm would then hope to gain additional profitable business again in the future. In fact, it might, at the time of submitting its low bid, be aware of some future profitable project it would receive that would more than offset the loss on the immediate contract.

In another situation, a seller may have some very attractive alternatives for its production capacity so it submits a very high bid. In this case, it keeps its name on the bidding list as being a responsive bidder. If it should by chance win the contract, it is assured of the business at a very good profit margin. Clearly, the particular circumstances of each firm regarding capacity, profitable alternatives, backlog of work, interest in future contracts and the objectives of management will have a great bearing on the bidding strategy of a seller at any given point in time.

One of the problems with the bidding process is that it provides an opportunity for sellers to "buy-in" to a program with a low bid price. This situation occurs primarily in the beginning of new projects or complex systems where little cost data is available and the design of the hardware may not be known. The contractor tends to underestimate the risks involved in the design and development stages. Consequently, in performing on the contract, the costs become greater than the bid price. The government then must choose between reimbursing the seller to forestall bankruptcy and thus keep him on the contract, or cancel the contract and forfeit all the development work done by the seller. Generally, the government opts to cover the excess costs and keep the firm on the project.

The Bidding Process

In order to submit a successful bid, a firm must make some estimates regarding competitive bids. Basically, the problem is one of correctly estimating the lowest bid price of your competitors so you may enter a winning bid. Several mathematical models and game theory have been used by many large firms to help solve the bidding problem.[1] The availability of a computer can be helpful in evaluating the many alternatives a bidder may choose. Without going into the sophisticated solutions that may be used, we shall discuss the general nature of the problem showing a basic approach to the solution.

Information about your competitors past bidding practices, fit of this procurement into their product lines, back-logs of their orders, utilization of their present capacity, and levels of cost can help in establishing a bid price on a potential contract. The nature of the product being purchased will affect the problem of determining the proper bid; however, the procedure will be essentially the same.

If the product is a standard commercial product, then the bidder has at least a market price as a guide for establishing his bidding range. Suppose a firm is bidding on a piece of office equipment that has been selling on the market competitively for $20.00. How might it evaluate its bidding alternatives?

The bidding firm in this case knows its cost of producing the item which at the proposed volume for the contract will be $15.00. A critical judgment that must be made by the bidder is the probable chance of winning the contract at prices lower than $20.00. One way of evaluating the situation is to determine a range of probabilities for the various prices and then develop a pay-off figure for each possible bid. The pay-off figure is found by multiplying the unit profit for each possible bid times the probability of the bidder's winning the contract at that bid. A typical situation for the proposed purchase of the office equipment might be represented as in Table 8-1.

Given the above profit per unit and the probabilities of winning the contract at the various bid prices, the pay-off would be the largest with a bid of $18.00 per unit. If the firm really needed the contract, it would be more sure of winning it if it submitted a bid of

$17.00 or something less. The lower the bid price, the greater the possibilities of winning the contract but with a lower profit margin. In the above case, any price above $15.00 would yield some profit to the firm. However, if the firm wanted to keep its plants running in order to retain certain types of employees because it anticipated better opportunities in the future, it might bid even less than the cost of $15.00 per unit.

TABLE 8-1
Different Bids and Resultant Pay-off

1 Bid Price	2 Unit Profit	3 Probability of Winning Contract	4 (2 x 3) Pay-off
$20	$5	.30%	$1.50
19	4	.50	2.00
18	3	.70	2.10
17	2	.90	1.80

In the above example, the critical judgment that must be made by management is the probability of getting the contract at each bid price. Obviously, the pay-off will change with a different set of probabilities. If the firm had other alternatives and did not really want the contract, it might bid $20.00 or even higher. Thus, if it did win the contract it would be at a good profit margin.

The more unique and specialized the product, i.e., one built to the buyer's specifications, the more difficult it is to judge the behavior of competitors. Competitors have different levels of operations and cost, and therefore may submit different bids even if they are expecting the same return on invested capital. No two firms are the same even in the same industry for their cost levels depend on their capacity, prices for materials and labor, skills of personnel, economies of scale, efficiency of operations, and the effectiveness of their management. The more unknowns involved in the situation, the more difficult it becomes to submit a winning bid that will meet the objectives of the bidding firm.

PRICING BY NEGOTIATION

Procurement by negotiation is used by governments and industrial buyers when they are unable to clearly specify the product or service to be purchased. If specification were possible, then the lowest price for the purchase could be secured through the formal advertising procedure utilizing competitive bidding.

In the negotiation method, the request for proposals is sent to pre-selected firms that are judged by the buyer to be capable of providing the end product. In the requests for proposals, the firm is given general specifications for the product, or asked to recommend to the buyer a combination of technology, product design, quality, complexity, etc., that will solve the customer's problem and give the buyer the best deal.

The firms responding to the proposal present their ideas about the kind of product required to solve the buyer's needs. Because of differences in design, quality, and specifications, the recommendations of the responding firms are not comparable and each must be evaluated by the buyer. If the buyer is interested in the product proposed by the firm, negotiation will take place to clarify the positions of both the buyer and seller. As negotiation proceeds, it becomes a process of bargaining between the buyer and seller.

What subjects are open for negotiation? The number and type of items that may be negotiated will depend upon the complexity of the procurement and the needs of the customer. Price is obviously one of the principal items of negotiation regardless of what is being purchased. But in the more complex procurements such as a weapons system for the Department of Defense or a space vehicle for the National Aeronautical Space Administration, or a high value, complex item for a state government, many things become eligible for negotiation.

When the buyer wants a product that represents the latest technology or state of the art in a given area, then the design, performance, and other characteristics of the end product will be considered during negotiation. Other topics for negotiation are: development of a prototype product, testing of the prototype; production and delivery schedules; spare parts; extra services to be provided such as training aids if required; additional or future buys; help from the buyer in getting scarce recources, materials, or manpower; plant and equipment to be provided by the buyer; follow-on work with other projects; technical capacity and competence; providing jobs in labor surplus areas; providing training programs for disadvantaged people; providing subcontracting opportunities for minority businesses; risks involved including those from changes in technology, cost forecasting, labor problems, and inflation; and finally, the type of contract to be written for the particular procurement. The above list includes only some of the things that come up in the negotiation sessions. How the selling firm responds to each item will depend upon the strategy he is following.

The Firm's Negotiation Strategy

Before a firm can start outlining a strategy for negotiation, it must clearly define its objectives and reasons for seeking a government contract. The objectives and reasons will vary by firm and may vary for a given firm over a period of time. Some of the stated reasons for selling to governments are listed below.

1. Make a profit on the sale of products or services.
2. Utilize excess plant capacity.
3. Increase volume to allow plant and equipment expansion.
4. Increase volume to lower per unit overhead charge and therefore increase profit on commercial business.
5. In slack periods try to retain professional people and skilled work force.
6. Develop new technology to be used later in commercial markets.
7. Get experience in Research and Development work with the government sharing in the cost.
8. Get initial contract and thus have an advantage in securing follow-on production runs.
9. Learn new technology and production skills.
10. Get government to furnish plant and/or equipment for the potential product.
11. Provide training ground for firm's personnel.
12. Firm can't transfer resources to another industry (out of defense work into commercial) and therefore has no alternative but to seek government contracts.

The above objectives of the firm will affect the negotiation strategy and the level of price that the firm will be willing to accept. For instance, if the firm has excess plant capacity and needs the additional volume of business to help cover its overhead, it will undoubtedly be less demanding at the negotiation table and settle for a moderate or a low price. On the other hand, if the firm has a back-log of orders and doesn't really care whether it gets the contract, then it will take a tougher bargaining position with regard to the total price, the type of contract, and extra services to be provided without charge.

Be Prepared

One department of the selling firm, or an individual in a small business, will be responsible for conducting the actual negotiations. Regardless of who is responsible, some very thorough preparation is required. The buyer's negotiator will be an experienced individual and will usually have specialized personnel such as lawyers, accountants, price and cost analysts, available to help him.

The value of the potential contract, the complexity of the procurement and its importance to the selling firm will influence the amount of preparedness required. A $100,000 contract for a firm doing $50,000,000 yearly sales will usually warrant a modest amount of preparation. However, again this depends on the firm's objectives. If the contract is in an area where the firm has not previously participated, it may prefer to over-prepare in order to insure winning the contract.

If the seller will be using a team of his own experts for the negotiations, then these people should be carefully selected and be properly briefed as to why the firm wants the particular contract and the type of trade-offs it can accept at the negotiation table.

If the firm has had previous experience negotiating contracts with the particular buyer, it should review those proceedings for guidelines as to potential problems and opportunities. Keeping a complete set of notes on each negotiation proceedings and the behavior of the buyer's negotiators can be very helpful when preparing for future negotiations. It may reveal how much emphasis a particular negotiator places on data, his penchant for following a time table, and his yield on small items, but firm stand on central issues. Any information such as this should be used in planning the negotiation strategy.

In preparing for the upcoming negotiation, the firm needs accurate and current data on technology, both their own and in the industry, cost estimates and forecasts, time tables for developing and testing prototype products, schedules for production and delivery, estimates of the rate of inflation for the life of the contract, and an evaluation of any other unknowns or risks that will affect contract performance. If the procurement under consideration is with the Federal government and covered by the Truth in Negotiations Act, then the firm must be prepared to supply the buyer with accurate, current, and complete cost and pricing date.

After all necessary data has been gathered, the firm must decide how it will price the contract. However, the price for the total procurement may be influenced by the type of contract to be written. In the preparation stage, the firm's "team" should review the possible incentive type contracts available for such a purchase and then integrate this information with their analysis of the total price.

If a large amount of development work is required, the firm might try to get two or more contracts for the total procurement. One contract would be on a cost-plus-incentive-fee basis for any required R & D work or work necessary to determine the feasibility of certain technologies. Another cost-plus-incentive-fee contract might be written to cover development and testing of a prototype product. Then, after the hardware has been tested and accepted and production is imminent, a fixed-price-incentive contract could be negotiated. This contract could then be based on the cost data developed during prototype development and testing.

Such contract considerations should be discussed by the firm's negotiating team during the preparation period. Any advantages and disadvantages to the firm should be clearly identified for future consideration during the negotiations.

If the contract being considered is for a large complex system, the firm must then gather data on the availability and cost of subcontractors. Such data would have to be available during the preparation stage if subcontracting is to be utilized.

Negotiations

By the date for negotiations, the seller's "team" should be thoroughly prepared and armed with the necessary back-up data. All "team" members should be briefed on the goals to be accomplished at the negotiation table, the maximum and minimum limits of price the firm can accept, and, if possible, some of the obvious trade-offs that are acceptable.

When negotiations start, the buyer will have reviewed the firm's proposals and supporting data. If several firms are being considered for the procurement, the buyer may then have an advantage when talking to each individual firm. He will be able to compare their designs, technologies, and prices. If required by law, the buyer will also have cost and pricing data from the firms. However, the buyer will not know the firm's reasons for seeking the contract, and thus can only guess how much the firm will give up in order to win the contract.

The negotiation process requires give-and-take on the part of both parties. But the firm should be ready for hard bargaining to secure certain goals that it feels are required if it is to perform successfully if awarded the contract. The firm should be as flexible as possible within the limits it has previously established.

Extracontractual influences such as the firm's reputation with regard to capability and reliability may play an indirect or even direct part in the negotiations. For example, if the firm has a reputation for always meeting time schedules for delivery, then the buyer will obviously not give the firm incentive payments for meeting the required delivery dates. Thus the seller must concentrate on getting incentive money for covering risks and other unknowns. Some other firm without such a good reputation might be given incentive pay to meet a particular delivery schedule. Even though it seems that the reputable firm is penalized in this instance, it should be recognized that a good reputation will in the long-run give the firm opportunities to be considered for a greater number of contracts, even though in specific instances it may affect the incentive pay available.

If negotiations are carried out over a period of weeks or months, the data should be constantly updated to compensate for any changes in variables or assumptions which influenced the original target price of the firm.

MARKETING AND CONTRACT PERFORMANCE

When the contract has been awarded to the firm, the responsibility for performance may be given to engineering, production, or some other department of the firm. The exact location for performance will be influenced by the nature of the work to be done, the size of the contract, and the size and organizational structure of the firm. Many decisions regarding marketing functions have already been spelled out in the contract. The type of product, production schedule, logistics and channel to be used, the price and terms of payment are all clearly stated in the contract. The marketing department must concentrate on market research, market intelligence, public relations, and market liaison by the personnel salesmen.

During the performance period, a salesman should become the liaison person between the buyer's office and the seller. Constant communication is necessary to learn of any changes in the needs of the customer with respect to the present contract. If such changes should be needed, then the contract may have to be modified through another negotiation session. Or, if options for the buyer were included in the contract, the buyer may decide to take advantage of them. Advance warning of such possibilities can be beneficial to the seller.

Periodical reports on the seller's progress should be communicated to the buyer. Any difficulties or disagreements should be discussed by the salesman and the buyer. The salesman should at all times strive to maintain a good, congenial working relationship with the buyer.

During the liaison period, the salesman should be developing leads on future projects of interest to the buyer, or projects contemplated by other government buyers. Returning to the buyer's office for discussions on the present contract offers good opportunities to learn of recent developments or future plans and needs of the government agencies. Marketing intelligence is an on-going activity and, if practiced by all salesmen on a conscientious basis, it can provide the seller with a valuable bank of data regarding anticipated projects and changes in the buyers' markets. The salesman should also be instructed to learn as much as possible about the availability of funds, for often this information leads to future project opportunities.

RENEGOTIATION

For some sellers supplying products to the Federal government, renegotiation is an ever present hazard. This constant threat of renegotiation should be a factor that the seller takes into consideration before, during, and after the negotiation of the original contract.

All firms that have contracts with the Department of Defense, National Aeronautical Space Administration, General Service Administration, Federal Aviation Administration, Atomic Energy Commission, and the Maritime Administration in the amount of $1 million or more are subject to the Renegotiation Act of 1951. In renegotiation cases, the Renegotiation Board is empowered to review the seller's performance on a contract *after* completion of the contract. If excess profits are found (and the Board defines what is excess profit) by the Board, the seller must reimburse the government for the amount of excess profits. The Board's decision can be appealed to the Court of Claims if the seller opposes the assessment of the Board.

The government procurement people defend the Renegotiation Act, stating that it has directly recouped more than $1 billion in excess profits since 1951.[2] Further, they believe it acts as a preventive measure and encourages sellers to price more accurately with respect to costs and thus avoid earning excess profits.

Sellers dealing with State and local government procurement agencies as well as with other Federal agencies do not have to be concerned with renegotiation at the present time. However, the Federal Commission on Government Procurement in 1972 recommended that the Renegotiation Act be extended to cover contracts of all Federal agencies, but to increase the base amount to $2 million in sales.[3]

For the selling firm, this seems to be a case where taking preventive measures may be the best strategy. However, even if the contract is a fixed-price contract and through a highly efficient operation a seller makes excess profits, such a contract can be opened for renegotiation if it is with one of the listed agencies. One of the obvious difficulties in devising a policy or strategy is the lack of any definitive statement by the government or Renegotiation Board clearly defining excess profits.

If the selling firm has to renegotiate a contract, it must present cost data to support its position that only normal profits were earned. Excess profits arise due to certain costs disallowed by the government, or, in some instances, through efficient operations or windfall situations, costs do not approach the level originally expected in a fixed-price contract. Clearly, the firm needs a good accounting system with proper accountability, recording and reporting of all costs. If the case is ultimately taken to the Court of

Claims, the firm should hire the best possible expert witness to help prove the appropriateness of the accounting methods and the proper allocation of costs.

MANAGING THE MARKETING ACTIVITY

By now, it should be clear that the government markets differ significantly from the consumer and industrial markets. Some of the government markets are large and highly oriented towards technology and large system purchases, especially the Federal markets of DoD, NASA, FAA, and AEC. Other customers tend to be concentrated geographically, and seek a wide range of products such as trucks, electronic equipment, aircraft, supplies for offices, construction services, maintenance repairs for equipment, and a great variety of other items. The buyers are professionals guided by laws and regulations. They are ever conscious of the fact that they are spending public funds which must be accounted for. The marketer must recognize and understand the peculiarities of these government markets and manage his marketing activities accordingly. Where the products and services are standard commercial items, the marketing manager may train his existing sales force to deal with this specific market. For the custom designed, non-standard items, marketing management and marketing techniques must be adapted to the environment of the special markets. Some of the problems of marketing management are dealt with in the following sections.

Need for Long-range Commitment

If the firm is interested in selling non-standard items to the government, then top management must commit resources to such operations for a long period of time. The firm must be organized to allow maximum communications and coordination between marketing and the other internal departments. Long range and short range objectives must be defined and used as guidelines for the development of policy for all levels of management.

Teams of experts are needed for bidding, negotiating, and performing on the special projects. It takes months or years to develop good working-teams; consequently, a long-range commitment is needed to collect on the ultimate pay-off. Many times, the firm has to bid on several contracts before it wins one. These bids may take place over a period of a year or so during which time adequate funds and business from other markets are needed.

If the firm expects to sell some of the more complex products and systems to the government, it will need substantial funds and experts to work up the necessary data to submit as their proposal in response to requests from government buyers. For example, the proposals for the B-1 air frame cost the potential sellers millions of dollars, some of which was repaid by the Federal government. The more specialized the product becomes, the more determined the commitment from management must be. Often, there are no alternative uses for the resources accumulated by the firm for producing weapon systems or other defense products. Thus, a firm cannot get into the specialized markets for a few years and then leave, without paying a heavy penalty in lost time and the loss of non-transferable resources.

Managing Marketing Communications

Much of the continued success of the firm in the government markets will depend on a well developed and managed internal and external marketing communications system. The internal system must be capable of collecting, sorting, and storing bits and pieces of information for later analysis to show overall trends and changes in markets. The system must include clear channels between marketing and the other internal departments such as finance, legal, accounting, engineering, production, and distribution. These departments must be constantly aware of the changing environment and the changing needs of the customers.

The external communications system must be established to facilitate marketing intelligence, marketing research, public relations, and advertising activities. The mix of the activities will depend to a large extent on the particular markets or customers.

Marketing management must concentrate on constantly gathering marketing intelligence. In this activity, the firm is concerned with any information regardless of the source if it will aid them in learning of new products and technology being considered by their customers, or being developed by competing firms. Marketing intelligence should be gathered about contracts that were awarded to competitors, and information on funds available for projects at the various levels of government. Such things as Congressional sentiment for solving the problems of the cities, or the determination of Congress to cut the defense budget should be covered. The purpose for gathering this information is to aid marketing management in evaluating changes in customers' needs and to search for new market opportunities.

After marketing intelligence has clearly indicated a new market opportunity, or a change in an old market, marketing research can be used to study the particular market in greater detail. It should determine who will be the customer, how much will be purchased of particular products, how to contact and sell the customer, and how soon funding will be available. Marketing research can be used for the in-depth studies that are needed to learn just how the firm's expertise and product lines can be used to solve the customer's needs.

Advertising and public relations have limited roles in government markets. Advertising may consist primarily of institutional advertising and participation in trade shows, or supplying information booths at conventions attended by members of the various buying organizations. Catalogues and direct-mail pieces are used for standardized products intended for government markets.

Public relations can be useful in making the buyers aware of the fact that the firm is involved in various markets and is constantly improving its technical capabilities. Public relations will be used most by the largest firms where efforts will be made to maintain good relations with editors of trade papers and other printed media. This is especially true of the firms in defense work who must overcome the anti-defense industry feelings that are quite popular in certain segments of society.

Generally, advertising and public relations are used sparingly because costs of such activities are not usually allowable costs of doing business with the Federal government. Consequently, such costs must be borne by business from the commercial sector or paid out of profits earned on government contracts.

Market Planning and Evaluation

Market planning and evaluation is a future oriented activity. In this activity, the data generated by research studies and information from marketing intelligence is used to evaluate future opportunities for the firm to capitalize on its unique expertise and product lines. During this process, the risks of winning certain contracts must be clearly enumerated. The government is a demanding buyer and some firms have found that they are forced to complete the contract even though it means gigantic losses. Input from the other line departments such as accounting, finance, engineering, legal, and production should be used to help evaluate and analyze the market opportunities and risks. The decision reached should be made jointly by all concerned areas of management and not left to a unilateral decision made by one area such as marketing.

Long range plans should be developed by marketing indicating where the strong marketing opportunities will be found in the future. Then, with counselling from other areas of management, marketing can develop plans of action to be used in the new markets. For such planning to be successful, top management must be sold on its value, and the plans developed must be more than general statements regarding hopes and aspirations.

Management of the Sales Function

The sales manager should coordinate and manage all the firm's sales activities. He should determine the best type of organizational structure for each particular market. Generally, large firms are organized in the field on a customer or product basis. The structure chosen should provide the firm with the best opportunity to serve the needs of the market.

In government markets where products are complex, or built to customer specification, the salesman must be either an engineer or have a high degree of technical ability. Small firms, because of limited funds, may be forced to rely entirely upon their engineers for contacts. However, a large firm can train a good salesman with respect to the technical aspects of the product and then furnish a team of engineering specialists to help in selling and explaining the more complex projects. In this case, the salesman must be a self-starter, have a good personality, and be good at working with others when selling or helping to negotiate a contract.

The basic duty of the salesman in the non-standard product government market is to sell the capabilities of his company. This means a constant sales effort on his part from the time he learns of a new project through the negotiation of a contract. Often the salesman has only a few government customers and has ample opportunity to learn all about their particular needs. Over many sales calls, he can become familiar with their behavior, interests, and prejudices while, at the same time, learning the important government regulations and Acts that govern the buyer's activities.

The salesman has total responsibility for gathering the marketing intelligence discussed in a previous section. He must constantly seek information on new projects, availability and timing of funds, as well as how funding is to be accomplished. He should know his competitor's products and contracts and be able to supply information to his marketing manager regarding any break-throughs in technology by competing firms. He must know the importance of gathering all types of information and know the best sources. In government markets as in other markets, the future success of the firm rests on how well the salesman understands and performs his job.

Customer Service

Some customer services must be provided by the seller during the performance on the contract and after the product has been delivered. If more than the normal amount of service will be necessary, then the type and amount should be specified in the cost of the contract.

Customer service must be effectively managed by the marketing department so that it accomplishes the necessary objectives, but does not constitute an uncontrolled expense that erodes profits. The seller may have to upgrade the training of the buyer's maintenance people to insure proper maintenance of the equipment. The seller may also have to work with the buyer to develop the proper inventory of parts and supplies.

The importance of customer service should never be under-estimated. Often the success of follow-up service on a contract will influence the buyer when awarding follow-on productions runs or awarding future contracts. The willingness on the part of the seller to help the customer in any way possible is often responsible for the reputation the seller gains in the market place. A good reputation for developing reliable, quality products, backed up by efficient customer service, is a great asset for any firm and can be a factor in securing future business in any market.

SUMMARY

Competitive bidding is a pricing technique used by a buyer to insure purchasing a product at the lowest possible price. Bidding is used in industrial markets as well as in government markets. The seller's success at bidding will depend upon his objectives for trying to win a contract as well as his estimate of the bids to be submitted by competitors.

Procurement by negotiation is used by buyers when they are unable to clearly specify the product or service to be purchased. In essence, the buyer states his problem or need in general terms in a "request for proposals" which is sent to selected sellers. The potential seller then responds by stating the type of product he would design and produce to meet the customer's needs. The buyer may then negotiate or bargain with all of the firms which responded until the buyer is satisfied that one seller's product is clearly superior to all others. Then, the buyer and the selected firm negotiate, among other things, the total price, production schedules, delivery schedules, and the type of contract to be written. Prior to negotiations, the seller must generate adequate data and make some judgments regarding the trade-offs he is willing to accept at the negotiation table. In negotiations for procurement of large complex systems, the seller will need help from his team of experts representing legal, accounting, finance, engineering, and production. The strategy the seller will follow will be largely determined by his objectives and reasons for seeking a government contract.

During the contract performance period, the engineering or production department will normally be given the responsibility for carrying out the terms of the contract. The salesman accepts the role of market liaison between the buyer and seller during the period of contract performance. The salesman must maintain close contact with the buyer to learn of any changes in the customer's needs which might influence the seller's performance on the contract.

Under certain conditions, the Renegotiation Board of the Federal government is empowered to review the completed contract searching for excess profits. If excess profits are found (and the Board defines in each case what constitutes excess profits), the seller must then reimburse the government for the amount claimed as excess profits. Certain legal recourse is available to the seller, but his best strategy is to control costs and pricing in such a way as to prevent the accumulation of excess profits. Renegotiation is one of the hazards a potential seller must recognize when doing business with certain Federal agencies.

When the seller decides to enter the non-standard product government market, it must be prepared to make a long period commitment of its resources. It takes time to develop the teams of experts necessary for negotiating, winning, and performing on many of the complex system contracts. Many firms that are participating in the defense market have no alternative uses for their specialized equipment and capabilities, and hence a long term commitment is mandatory for these firms.

The major marketing activities to be performed in the government markets are marketing communications, marketing intelligence, market research, market liaison, market planning and evaluation, and follow through with a responsive customer service function.

Selling the company's capabilities is the salesman's primary duty until after the contract has been won. Then, gathering information and intelligence about future markets and opportunities becomes his major responsibility. After the information has been collected by the marketing department, specific plans for capitalizing on the future opportunities should be developed. Although marketing is responsible for the specific plans, all major decisions should be coordinated with the other departments of the firm. The ultimate specific plans must reflect the best judgment of management at all levels of the firms regarding which future opportunities should be explored.

FOOTNOTES

1. For information on bidding see: H. W. Boyd, Jr. and W. F. Massy, *Marketing Management*, (New York: Harcourt Brace Jovanovich, Inc., 1972), pp. 337-340.; P. Kotler, *Marketing Decision Making*, (New York: Holt, Reinhart and Winston, 1971), pp. 348-53.; F. D. Sturdivant, et al, *Managerial Analysis in Marketing*, (Glenview, Ill.: Scott, Foresman and Co., 1970), pp. 487-94.

2. *Report of the Commission on Government Procurement*, Superintendent of Documents, Washington, D.C., 1972, Vol. 4., p. 189.

3. Ibid., p. 189.

QUESTIONS

1. Why is bidding the preferred pricing technique in government markets?

2. What strategies might a seller follow when bidding for a contract?

3. What factors will influence his choice of strategy? Why?

4. Why is it difficult for a seller to win a contract by bidding and maximize his profit at the same time?

5. Under what conditions and circumstances is negotiation a preferred pricing method in government markets? Why?

6. Why do the objectives of the firm affect the seller's negotiation strategy?

7. What data does a seller collect just prior to beginning negotiations?

8. What is marketing's role in the contract performance stage?

9. What is renegotiation? Why is it considered a hazard when negotiating a contract with the Federal government?

10. Why is there a need for a long-range commitment on the part of a seller in the defense industry?

11. Discuss the role of marketing intelligence for a firm selling products to the Department of Defense.

12. What is the role of the marketing department in market planning and evaluation?

13. How does the salesman's role differ in the government market from his role in the industrial market?

14. What is the role of customer service in the highly technical market of the Federal Aviation Administration (consider the sale of an automatic landing system for airports)?

SMALL BUSINESS: MARKETING
OPPORTUNITIES AND
ASSISTANCE PROGRAMS

Small business firms can find many opportunities to sell their products and services to procurement agencies at all levels of Federal government. In fact, because these firms are small, or owned by minority people, they are eligible for many federal programs that can help them develop their firm.

Full and free competition is stimulated by the federal government with interest in all qualified suppliers regardless of size. However, recognizing that small business firms are often at a disadvantage compared to large firms, many marketing opportunities are often reserved for small and minority businesses. Specific federal programs are designed to help the small firms take advantage of these marketing opportunities. This chapter explains how many of the more important federal programs for small and minority businesses operate.

WHAT IS A SMALL BUSINESS?

Nearly everyone agrees that the five-man machine shop or the corner food store would be considered small businesses. But when we consider other businesses that employ hundreds of people or have receipts of several million dollars, it is less clear as to whether or not they should be given the status of a small business or considered a medium sized business. There are no universal yardsticks for measuring smallness or bigness that apply equally to all industries. In the wholesale industry, a firm with 150 people may dominate the industry, whereas a manufacturing firm employing 300 people may be very small for that particular industry.

During the 1940's, Congress tried to define small business through legislation but finally gave up and in 1953, when writing the Small Business Act, stated that the Small Business Administration (SBA) had the responsibility to define a small business in each of the various industries. Since 1953, the size of a small business as stipulated by the SBA has changed, with the trend towards raising the upper limits of size in various industries.

For the purposes of making loans, SBA has defined a small business in four major fields of activity. These definitions are used by many other federal agencies and institutions when they wish to identify small businesses, and in lieu of more acceptable criteria, they tend to be accepted as universal definitions. They are as follows:[1]

1. Wholesaling — annual receipts from $5 million to $15 million depending on the industry.
2. Retail or Service — annual receipts from $1 million to $5 million, depending on the industry.
3. Construction — annual receipts of not more than $5 million, averaged over a three-year period.
4. Manufacturing — from 250 to 1,500 employees depending on the industry.

The need for a clear definition of a small business is to help determine which firms in a particular industry are entitled to the various aids and services of the Small Business Administration and other federal agencies.

THE ROLE OF THE SMALL BUSINESS ADMINISTRATION

The Small Business Administration (SBA) was created by Congress in 1953 and it became a permanent government agency in 1958.[2] The purposes of the Small Business Administration are to: Aid, counsel, assist, and protect the interests of small business; insure that small business concerns receive a fair proportion of Government purchases, contracts, and subcontracts, as well as of the sales of Government property; make loans to small business concerns, State and local development companies, and the victims of floods or other catastrophes; license, regulate and make loans to small business investment companies; improve the management skills of small business owners, potential owners, and managers; and conduct studies of the economic environment.

In order to better serve the eight million small businesses in the country, the SBA has encouraged the participation of business, academic, financial and management segments in its various studies and programs. It has more recently focused attention and assistance on the low-income and other disadvantaged groups.

General Programs

The SBA has a number of programs of financial and management assistance for small businesses. Some of the more important ones are:

1. Business loans (either participating with a bank or guaranteeing up to 90 percent of the loan) for business construction or expansion, purchase of machines, equipment, or materials and working capital.

2. Equal Opportunity Loans for the disadvantaged business-man or woman.

3. Development company loans at the State or local level to expand the economy by promoting and assisting the development of small business concerns.

4. Disaster Loans necessitated by disasters — storms, floods, earthquakes or other catastrophes.

5. Lease guarantee programs to aid small businessmen in leasing good locations for their businesses.

6. Surety Bond programs for helping small contractors as well as subcontractors supplying products and services.

7. Minority Enterprise programs designed to make more sound business opportunities available to minority individuals.

8. Small business investment companies (SBIC's) which help finance small business firms.

9. Procurement assistance to aid small businesses in getting a larger share of the Federal Government business through prime contracts and subcontracts (this will be discussed more in detail later in this chapter)

10. Management assistance through courses, workshops, conferences, clinics, and individual counseling.

11. Advisory Councils for communication between SBA and citizens in each area of the country. They report on the small business climate and make suggestions and recommendations to SBA for programs and services that will better meet the needs of the small business man or woman.

The SBA provides several series of management, marketing and technical publications for managers of small businesses. Some of these are free while others must be purchased. The free management assistance publications are listed under the headings of *Management Aids, Technical Aids,* and *Small Business Bibliographies.* These can be secured by mail from an SBA field office or from the Washington Office. A number of other more extensive studies have been published in booklet form and can be purchased from the Superintendent of Documents Government Printing Office in Washington D.C. 20402. These booklets are in the following series: *Small Business Management Series,* (covering such topics as marketing, cost accounting, ratio analysis for small business), *Starting and Managing Series,* (more in-depth studies of cash planning, growth and survival in the first two years), and *Aid Annuals,* (yearly publications on aids for marketers, small business, and manufacturers).

After reviewing the above list of publications and programs, it is apparent that the SBA has developed a comprehensive series of aids and services that can be extremely valuable to an established or potential small business.

SMALL BUSINESS ADMINISTRATION
AND GOVERNMENT PROCUREMENT

The Federal Government, working through the SBA, provides special aids and programs designed to help small business get a larger share of the volume of purchases made by the various federal agencies. Although the programs are to help small business sell more to the federal government, many of the aids may indirectly help a small business sell to state and local government organizations as well as to other industries. Some of the major programs will be discussed in detail in the following sections.

Set-Asides

One of the major programs relating to federal procurement is the "set-aside" program. It is designed to help small business get a bigger share of government purchases and thereby enlarge the indsutrial base of the country and increase opportunities for greater competition for government business.

There are two types of "set-asides" for small business. The first is called a "joint set-aside" which is authorized under the Small Business Act. In this case, a representative of SBA working with the procuring agency makes the decision as to what and and how much of the intended procurement will be "set-aside" for small business. This type is used most and receives constant attention from the SBA representatives to insure that all potential procurements receive their consideration. This program, although often discouraged by contracting officers of the procurement agency, has been responsible for providing unprecedented opportunities for small businesses during the past two decades.

The second type is a "unilateral set-aside" which is made by the procuring agency during periods of national emergency. During an emergency, it is necessary to expand the production capacity of the country as rapidly as possible. Under these conditions, all potential suppliers, both large and small, are automatically considered by the procuring agencies. Usually no pressure is needed under these conditions to channel procurement contracts to small businesses.

In either of the above situations, the "set-aside" may be total or partial. If it is a total "set-aside", then only small businesses can be used as suppliers. Where the procurement is for a product that can be separated into two or more production runs, part of it is often restricted to small business only. Then all interested firms may bid on the unrestricted portion. All small firms whose bids were less than 130 percent of the highest award winning bid are then offered the restricted part of the procurement at the highest price paid on the unrestricted part.

Besides the above programs, some procuring agencies select certain items or services which are procured only from small business. Construction contracts of less than $500,000 are often reserved for small contractors. The Department of Defense also has a program of mandatory "set-asides" of appropriate products for small businesses located in "labor surplus areas."

Certificates of Competency

Often the procuring agency does not believe the small business firm with the lowest bid on a contract has the capacity, credit, or capability to perform satisfactorily on the contract. In this instance, the procuring agency must submit the case to the Small Business Administration who conducts an investigation of the small business firm.

The SBA representative makes a complete on-site study of the facilities, management, performance record and financial status of the firm. If the firm meets all the requirements of SBA, then a Certificate of Competency is issued to the firm by SBA for that particular contract. If the firm is deficient in some area, such as lacking in financial capability, the SBA may make arrangements to help the firm overcome the problem and then issue the Certificate of Competency.

If the SBA decides favorably for the firm and issues a Certificate of Competency, it must be accepted by the procurement officer of the procuring agency. The Small Business Act dictates this policy stating Government procurement officers " . . . are directed to accept such certification (from SBA) and are authorized to let such Government contracts to such concern or group of concerns without requiring it to meet any other requirement with respect to capacity and credit."[3]

Subcontracting

When the government awards a contract to a contractor for the production of a product or service, such a contract is referred to as a *prime* contract. The contractor, or seller in this case, has worked directly with the government procurement agency to secure the contract. The contract may be a negotiated contract, or one won through being the lowest bidder on a formal advertised procurement action.

Often the contract covers a major weapons system which requires technical capability and plant capacity far exceeding that of the contractor or seller who signed the prime contract. In such a circumstance, the contractor holding the prime contract will negotiate with other business firms, either large or small, who have the expertise and plant capability to produce a certain part or portion of the weapons system, called for in the prime contract. Eventually, the prime contractor will sign a *subcontract* with the other firm, or firms, for the production of a specific item or a part of the weapons system. Thus, subcontractors become an important part of the government's procurement process.

In 1970, an estimated fifty cents out of every Department of Defense prime contract dollar went to subcontractors. An earlier DoD review showed that the top ten prime contractors subcontracted an average of 54 percent of their contract dollars.[4] In the Apollo program of NASA, only a few of the 20,000 companies included in the program were prime contractors; the remainder were subcontractors.

The statutes and procurement regulations of the government (Armed Services Procurement Regulations and the Federal Procurement Regulations) do not spell out the relationship of the subcontractor to the prime contractor nor do they give much attention to subcontracts. In fact, subcontractors seldom enjoy the benefits of the prime contractor such as advance and progress payments, or speedy redress against the government for the termination of a particular contract. The subcontractor must look to the prime contractor for relief in such circumstances.

In many instances, different federal government agencies have different policies with regard to the review and approval of subcontractors. This often works a hardship on those subcontractors in the small business category. Delays in settlements are commonplace especially when the subcontractor's termination claim must be processed through several tiers of subcontractors up to the prime contractor and finally to the procuring agency.

Regardless of the problems inherent in the present methods of handling subcontracts, many profitable opportunities in the subcontracting field are often overlooked by small business firms. Department of Defense contracts in the amount of $500,000 or more, having substantial subcontracting possibilities, require that the prime contractor maintain a Defense Small Business Subcontracting and Labor Surplus Area Program. Such contractors are required to designate a Small Business Liaison Officer who administers the company subcontracting program for small businesses. These programs are designed to assist small business firms and to afford them opportunities to participate in Defense work as subcontractors. The

Commerce Business Daily is useful in identifying firms which offer subcontracting opportunities.

In keeping with this national policy, NASA cooperates with the Department of Commerce and the Small Business Administration to help small firms and minority business enterprises participate in the NASA procurement programs. In fiscal year 1972, NASA reported subcontracts totaling $391 million out of a total of $2,195 millions awarded to prime contractors. The subcontracts were being performed by 1,083 different first and second-tier subcontractors. These subcontracts were being performed in 505 cities in 43 states, and 730 small business concerns received $62 million, or 16 percent of the total subcontract dollars.[5]

The Small Business Administration works closely with procurement offices of the Department of Defense, General Services Administration, National Aeronautics and Space Administration, Atomic Energy Commission, Federal Aviation Administration and other agencies to uncover possible contracting opportunities for small businesses.

In 1972, seventy-six contractors for the Department of Defense subcontracted a total of $9.9 billion with 34.8 percent of this amount going to small business subcontractors. This percentage has declined from a high of 43.3 percent in 1967, but has remained constant at 34.8 percent for the past two years. There is no way to determine whether such a percentage is good or bad.

The Navy has experimented with a mandatory subcontracting program for small businesses in the development of the MK 56 mine. The prime contractor was

> required to place first-tier subcontracts equal to 25 percent of the total contract price with small firms; to identify proposed first-tier small business subcontractors; to describe the subcontracted items; and to estimate in dollars the value of the subcontracts. The Navy reported that this subcontracting requirement did not increase prime contract costs, that the prime contractor awarded more than the prescribed 25 percent and that the mandatory provision did not diminish overall competition.[6]

Some authorities on federal government procurement believe that during peace-time when the Department of Defense budgets are reduced, it may be necessary to use a mandatory subcontracting program such as described above, in order to increase, or even just stabilize, the present share of subcontracts going to small business.

To encourage more small businesses to seek prime and subcontracts with the federal government, the SBA works with local business groups and other government agencies in meetings and conferences where small businessmen can learn of such opportunities. The government procuring offices and prime contractors present their needs and requirements at these meetings and discuss the bidding opportunities with interested small businessmen. Information regarding such future meetings can be secured from the SBA field offices throughout the country.

The SBA representatives also moniter future purchases of DoD, NASA, GSA, AEC, and other agencies to find procurement actions on which few small businesses have responded in the past. If it is believed that small businesses could and should be getting a share of such business, the SBA personnel will search for local small businesses that might be interested in bidding for the contracts. If the businessman is unfamiliar with federal procurement procedures, the SBA representative counsels him on how to sell to the government. This service is provided in the SBA field offices as well as in the SBA offices that are maintained at military and other major federal procurement offices.

SMALL PURCHASE PROCEDURE OF
THE FEDERAL GOVERNMENT

Many small businessmen in the locality of military bases or other offices of federal agencies and department, can very easily and effectively compete in gaining a profitable share of the "small purchase" business of the federal government. For classification purposes, the federal government classifies purchases in one single transaction of goods and services of less than $2,500, and construction contracts of less than $2,000, as small purchases.

There are currently four simplified, primary methods of making small purchases that are used by the military services and other organizations related to the Department of Defense. Other government agencies use similar methods, or variations of these, depending upon the circumstances surrounding the purchase.

The four methods used by DoD are: (1) blanket purchase agreements, (2) imprest funds (petty cash funds), (3) purchase orders, and (4) U.S. Government National Credit Card. Oral solicitation of prices and other information is used to decrease administration costs. Most routine small purchases are handled by a buyer under the direction of the base or agency contracting officer. Businessmen find this method of procurement easy to deal with because it involves very little paper-work. Becasue of this, it is easier for the government to get more suppliers interested in these small purchases. This results in greater competition and the government buyer is more assured of the right quality product at the lowest possible price.

Much of the federal governments yearly purchasing activity is related to the procurement of small purchases. In Fiscal year 1967, approximately eight million purchasing actions were under $2,500, representing an expenditure of $1.8 billion. It has been estimated that the administrative expense of making a multiple award under a solicitation (formal advertising) is at least $50.00.[7] For many small purchases, the cost of making the procurement using advertising was greater than the value of the product or service being purchased. Thus, for most small purchases, the government has simplified its purchasing procedures so that they are now substantially like those found in industry.

MINORITY BUSINESS OPPORTUNITIES AND PROGRAMS

According to information from the Department of Commerce in 1969, the latest data available, there were 322,000 minority-owned businesses representing about 4.3 percent of the total number of businesses in the country. The total receipts for these minority owned businesses were $10.6 billion or approximately .7 percent of the receipts reported by all firms.[8] The data further indicated that minority owned businesses are heavily concentrated in small retail and service activities. Minorities, constituting 17 percent of the total U.S. population, own or control only a small portion of the businesses in the U.S. In the past few years, several federal programs have been implemented towards alleviating the situation.

"Minority business enterprise" means a business enterprise that is owned or controlled by one or more socially or economically disadvantaged persons. Such disadvantage may arise from cultural, racial, chronic economic circumstances or background or other similar cause. Such persons include, but are not limited to, Negroes, Puerto Ricans, Spanish-speaking Americans, American Indians, Eskimos, and Aleuts.[9]

There are two major Federal government programs developed for promoting marketing and business opportunities for minority businesses. One program is under the jurisdiction of the Small Business Administration and the other is managed by the Office of Minority Business Enterprise in the Department of Commerce. Outlays for these minority business programs have expanded from $213 million in 1969 to a projected $716 million in 1973. Both of the above programs will be discussed in the following sections.

Small Business Administration Programs
for Minority Businesses

Under the provisions of Section 8(a) of the Small Business Act (Public Law 85-536), the SBA may enter into contracts with DoD,

NASA, or other government agencies for supplies and services and, in turn, award subcontracts to small business concerns who are unable to bid competitively on the procurement. In this instance, the SBA is the prime contractor for the supplies or services and can determine which business firms will be awarded subcontracts. DoD, NASA, and other government agencies help to identify products and services that are appropriate for contracts to small firms under the 8(a) Section of the Act. This is one way in which the SBA can expand participation of eligible disadvantaged people in business ownership and federal procurement actions.

An important factor in eligibility is qualification as a disadvantaged person. Such persons, through no fault of their own, have been deprived of the opportunity to compete effectively in the economy. The business firm that is awarded the subcontract from SBA can be a sole proprietorship, owned by the disadvantaged person; a partnership with at least 50 percent of the ownership belonging to a disadvantaged person; or a corporation with at least 51 percent of the present and future stock owned by a disadvantaged individual. In the case of a partnership or corporation, at least one officer must be a disadvantaged person employed full time in a key position.

The goal of the Section 8(a) program is to provide government contracting opportunities to minority businesses who normally would be unable to bid on competitive contracts. Any minority firm interested in such opportunities should contact their nearest SBA field office, or the SBA office at the nearest military establishment.

Procurement opportunities for minority firms are not limited to the Section 8(a) programs. If the minority firm has the capacity and capability to compete, it can bid on any government contract.

Under the Section 8(a) program, minority firms increased their sales to the Federal government from $8 million in fiscal year 1969 to $66 million in fiscal year 1971. The total sales to the federal government by minority businesses on a direct competitive basis (those not in the Section 8(a) program) increased from $12.7 million in fiscal year 1969 to $141.7 million in fiscal year 1971.[10]

The SBA also operates the Minority Enterprise Program where SBA representatives cooperate with local community groups and explain to potential and present owners of minority businesses how the SBA programs can help them achieve business success. The SBA will advise on any matter related to the business, but studies of management materials for private surveys have shown that inadequate management is the cause of 90 percent of the new business failures.

To help finance the minority business, the normal loan criteria are relaxed by SBA, but emphasis is placed on the character of owners and the possibility of repayment out of the profits of the business.

Minority loans approved by SBA were $86 million in 1969; $195 million in 1971; $332 (est) million in 1972; and $452 (est) million for 1973.[11] The average loan is for approximately $28,000 and for an average repayment period of five to six years.[12]

There has been substantial improvements in the volume of procurement dollars going to minority businesses in the past five years. This volume of business helps the firm to grow and gain experience which can be applied to markets at other levels of government or to the commercial markets. Other indirect benefits from these SBA and federal programs should become apparent in the future. Inasmuch as many minority firms tend to employ disadvantaged people, the economic status of such people should continue to improve along with the increased volume of business enjoyed by minority firms.

Office of Minority Business Enterprise

The Office of Minority Business Enterprise (OMBE) and the National Advisory Council on Minority Business Enterprise were established in the Department of Commerce by Executive Order 11458, on March 5, 1969. The order charged the Secretary of Commerce to foster and promote minority business enterprise by (a) coordinating all Federal minority enterprise programs, (b) mobilizing private resources, and (c) establishing an information center. The President charged the Council to advise the Secretary in those efforts. Each Federal Agency and Department was made responsible for cooperating with the Secretary in the performance of his functions.

The present Office of Minority Business Enterprise operates under the Authority of Executive Order 11625 issued October 13, 1971. The early order 11458 was continued and the new order 11625 gave the Secretary of Commerce, and through him the OMBE, increased authority over all Federal Activities in the minority enterprise field. The Secretary was given a clear mandate to establish and carry out Federal policy concerning minority enterprise and to coordinate the related efforts of all Federal Departments and agencies. It also directed the departments and agencies to develop systematic data collection processes concerning their minority enterprise programs and to cooperate in expanding the overall Federal effort.[13]

In the past two years, the OMBE has developed many programs to aid present and potential owners of minority businesses. It has sponsored the development of The Minority Business Associations which benefit the individual businessman at the local level. OMBE has developed 130 Business Development Organizations in local communities which are staffed with experienced business professionals who help start the minority businesses.

The OMBE has helped develop Business Resource Centers in local communities to aid in mobilizing, coordinating, and deploying the resources of the business community in support of local minority business development. The Centers assure the availability of equity capital and seek expanded markets and sales opportunities for the minority businesses.

The OMBE through its Task Force on Education and Training is promoting a Minority Youth Awareness program designed to inform minority high school children and other children of the rewards and risks of owning their own business. Other programs finance technical and management assistance, defray costs of pilot or demonstration projects, and publish information on private programs assisting minority businesses in the large cities and offer information on franchise opportunities.

Although the above OMBE programs are not directly related to the marketing of products to governments, they will directly affect the availability and capability of minority businesses in the future. With the success of these programs, coupled with the SBA Section 8(a) program, more minority businesses will be able to effectively compete for the opportunities to sell products and services to governments at all levels.

DoD PROGRAMS FOR SMALL BUSINESS AND LABOR SURPLUS AREA[14]

The Department of Defense programs listed below are utilized in the Army, Navy, Air Force, and Defense Supply Agency. Small business specialists at the procurement offices of each of the above agencies are available to assist businessmen in obtaining information and guidance on Defense procurement procedures, how to be placed on the bidder's mailing list, and identification of both prime and subcontract opportunities. The programs are as follows:

1. Prime Contractor Source Development and Utilization.
    This program is developing, listing, screening, for IFB (bid) action and RFP (proposal) action, and thereafter using the developed small business and labor surplus area sources. This source development generates the "prime" contracting program for small business and labor surplus areas.

2. Small Business and Labor Surplus Preference Activities
    Here "partial" and "total" set-asides as authorized by law, are used for small business concerns; and "partial" set-asides are used for labor surplus area concerns.

3. Subcontracting Procedures and Practices.

Program carried on with prime contractors to insure that small business concerns and labor surplus area concerns are utilized in subcontracting. These consist of special clauses for utilization in prime contracts, prime contractor workshops, plant visits to major prime contractors, and liaison activities with Small Business Administration.

4. Small Business and Labor Surplus Area Procurement Conferences.

These are held on a DoD-wide, on a service (Army, Navy, Air Force, Defense Supply Agency), and on procurement office basis to acquaint small business and labor surplus area concerns on the federal contract process. This action is by presentations, discussions, films, suitcase-type exhibits, and pass-out materials.

5. Counsel and Assistance

This action involves maintenance of bid rooms, or lists of "buy items", advanced planning lists, interpretations, financing, facilities assistance, introduction of potential contractors to the pertinent "buy" agency, checking of delivery schedules, furnishing of informative data, and assistance on securing of specifications and drawings.

6. Special Projects

Programs in which the small business, labor surplus area, and economic utilization expertise is of assistance. This would include assistance on training programs for small business and economic utilization personnel; and advanced industry briefings, and work on economic studies.

To facilitate the use of the programs by small business firms, the Department of Defense publishes in booklet form the location of Army, Navy, Air Force, and Defense Supply Agency procurement and contact administration offices and the names of the small business specialists alphabetically by state.

FEDERAL AGENCIES HELP SMALL BUSINESSES

The agencies of the Federal government are aware of the Minority Programs and interest of the Federal government in developing minority businesses. Each in its own way is making its contribution to the success of the programs.

The activities at the Goddard Space Flight Center are an example of what is being done by one agency to improve the opportunities of small and minority businesses.

Goddard has developed programs and conferences designed to attract the interest of minority businesses. The Industry Assistance Section of the Procurement Division maintains a file of minority businesses that can supply a wide range of services such as construction, data processing, electronics, keypunch, machine shop, microcircuits, management system evaluation, printed circuits, research and development, and technical writing. To date, such firms have provided Goddard with valuable services in computer program maintenance, machine shop equipment maintenance, lawn care and off-site duplicating.

A designated employee acts as Goddard's liaison and coordinator for minority business opportunities. She contacts Goddard technical offices to locate areas where minority firms might be of service to the Center under the provision of Section 8(a) of the Small Business Act.[15]

The various division and technical areas at Goddard participate in procurement fairs, seminars, and conferences at Goddard, Baltimore, and Washington, D.C. to inform minority businesses in the local area about the products and services Goddard is interested in procuring. Sometimes Goddard puts on a series of demonstrations at the Center showing the product lines of the minority firms to expose the Goddard technical people to a company's capability. As a result of these efforts, Goddard has witnessed an increase in the contracts and subcontracts placed with minority firms in the past year. In fiscal year 1973, Goddard placed $1.9 million in Section 8(a) contracts which was nearly double that of previous years.

It is clear the Federal government is interested in helping small business firms develop into effective and efficient competitors.

Last year, the Small Business Office of the Space and Missile Systems Organization of the Air Force taught eighteen Los Angeles small businessmen, in a thirteen-week course, the basic procedures for competing for government contracts. It was part of a pilot program designed to generate more interest among small business firms in selling products and services to the government.

The course was taught by a procurement specialist with participation from other experts explaining such topics as the Small Business Administration, special programs for small business firms, types of contracts, labor laws, bonds, insurance, and taxes.

Such efforts as this are duplicated each year by many procurement offices in the DoD agencies. Last year, seven Air Force Systems Command Field procurement organizations won awards from the Secretary of the Air Force for exceeding their small business and minority enterprise goals for the year.

The programs discussed above offer unparalleled opportunities for small business and minority enterprises. Through these programs, they can develop their capabilities and grow large enough to compete not only for federal government business, but can sell their products and services to other governments and industries.

SUMMARY

There are many marketing opportunities for small and minority business firms to supply products and services to procurement agencies at all levels of government. In order to help small and minority business firms take advantage of these opportunities, the Federal government has developed many specialized programs which are under the direction of the Small Business Administration and the Office of Minority Business Enterprise.

Perhaps the most important federal program for providing marketing opportunities for small and minority businesses is the "set-aside" program. In this program, either the total, or a partial, amount of the intended procurement action is "set-aside" for small and minority business participation. In the event that the small or minority firms are not capable of serving as a prime contractor, Section 8(a) of the Small Business Act authorizes the Small Business Administration to serve as the prime contractor and then subcontract the procurement to eligible small and minority firms.

Besides the above program, the small purchase business of the Federal government and other governments, is available for small and minority business firms. The Federal government has taken steps to simplify the small purchase procedure, thereby encouraging more small firms to compete which results in better prices for the government.

Generally, the Federal government has done more than other levels of government to encourage small and minority firms to participate in government business. The Department of Defense, National Aeronautical and Space Administration, and other Federal procurement agencies have specific programs for helping small and minority businesses. In the past several years, the small and minority business firms have supplied an ever increasing amount of products and services to the federal government.

FOOTNOTES

1. *SBA What it is . . . What it does,* U.S. Small Business Administration, Washington, D.C. 1972. (More detailed definitions are set forth in Section 121.3-10 of Part 121, Chapter I, Title 13 of the

Code of Federal Regulations.)

2. Small Business Act 1953, (67 Stat. 232) U.S. Gov't. Organizational Manual, 1972-73, Gov't. Printing Office, Wash. D.C., p. 496.

3. Small Business Act, 72 Stat. 391; U.S.C. 5637 (1970).

4. As quoted in *Report of the Commission on Government Procurement*, Government Printing Office, Washington D.C. 1972, Volume 1, p. 88.

5. *Annual Procurement Report*, National Aeronautics and Space Administration, Washington, D.C., Fiscal Year 1972. p. 3.

6. *Report of the Commission on Government Procurement*, Government Printing Office, Washington, D.C. Dec. 1972, Volume 1 p. 132.

7. *Small Purchase Manual*, Armed Services Procurement Regulation, ASPM No. 2., Dec. 1969, Department of Defense, Wash., D.C., p. 1.

8. U.S. Bureau of the Census, *Statistical Abstract of the United States: 1972*, (93rd Edition) Washington, D.C., 1972, p. 471-472.

9. Executive Order 11625, 13 October 1971, Washington, D.C. Section 6, para (a).

10. *Highlight Accomplishments*, Office of Minority Business Enterprise, Washington, D.C., 13 October 1971.

11. *The Budget of the U.S. Government, 1973*, Government Printing Office, Washington, D.C., 1973. p. 120

12. *SBA What is it*, U.S. Small Business Administration Washington, D.C., 1972. p. 6.

13. *Press release*, Office of the White House Press Secretary, Washington, D.C. 13 October 1971.

14. This section is based on *Small Business and Labor Surplus Area Specialists*, Department of Defense, Washington, D.C. 20301.

15. Taken from *Goddard News*, Goddard Space Flight Center, Greenbelt, Maryland, Nov. 1972.

QUESTIONS

1. Why is it so difficult to define a "small business"?

2. Why is the Federal government interested in having small and minority businesses compete for government business?

3. Discuss the importance of the general programs of the SBA with regards to a small machine shop located near a prime contractor for a space vehicle.

4. What is the "set-aside" program? Why is it important to small business firms?

5. What is a "Certificate of Competency"? Why are they important?

6. Explain the mechanics and importance of subcontracting.

7. What is the role of SBA in subcontracting? Do you think SBA should function as a prime contractor? Why or why not?

8. Explain the small purchase procedure of the Federal government.

9. How can small and minority business firms gain a greater share of the small purchase business?

10. What is the role of OMBE?

11. Specifically, how do the Small Business Administration programs aid minority businesses?

12. Sumamrize the major small and minority business programs and give your overall evaluation of their success.

The previous chapters have served to illustrate several important aspects about federal procurement: It is massive in size, complex in its administration, pervasive in its effect on the economy, and scrutinized by everyone. Congress is sensitive to all these aspects and when a chorus of complaints about procurement came from many points in the 1960's, it decided a full-scale study of the procurement process was necessary.

Congress was the logical body to do the study since it is both author and controller of the procurement process. It creates the purchasing statutes, passes on the national budget submitted by the President, funds needed actions, and is the recipient of the reports from multiple agencies that watch-dog the purchasing. Federal procurement personnel, business firms, members of Congress, and the public criticized the process as being cumbersome, inequitable, and inefficient. The process has grown in a patchwork way since 1949 to handle huge programs such as the space and military systems. By 1966, it became apparent to Congress that rather than more patchwork, a full-scale study and total revamping of the statutory and regulatory machinery was necessary.

In 1969, Public Law 91-129 was passed by Congress and the study began under the chairmanship of Representative Chet Holifield. Concluded in 1972, the report filled four volumes and contained 149 recommendations for changes.

The Commission Report is both insightful and wide-ranging in its scope. Its potential for future changes makes it highly significant for marketers. How firms do business with federal agencies in the future will undoubtedly change. For this reason, the study is included in this book and is the basis for this chapter on the future for selling to the federal government.

DEVELOPMENT OF THE COMMISSION AND ITS REPORT

As Figure 10-1 suggests, Congress had the feeling in the late 1960's that their huge expenditures for programs, particularly military missions and systems, had created a jungle of complexity and inefficiency. Spurred by the publicity surrounding the cost-overruns

FIGURE 10-1
"Faster — I Think It's Gaining On Us"

Source:　Reprinted by permission of *The Washington Post*, Washington, D.C., Jan.
12, 1972 p. A15.

of the Lockheed C5-A, the TFX fighter aircraft, and failure of several other military programs to prove fruitful, Congress authorized creation of *The Commission on Government Procurement.* The Commission noted, for example, that the statutory basis for federal buying " ... is a welter of disparate and confusing contradictions and of grants of limited authority to avoid the restrictions."[1]

Objectives and Scope

The twelve member Commission had as its main mission recommendation of ways to achieve the policy goals of Congress for the *entire* procurement system, not only the military purchases. The general objectives were the same as stated in 1775 when the Second Continental Congress created the Commissary General to obtain the services and products for the federal government; maximize competition for contracts, obtain reasonable prices, and assure the accountability of public officials for the transactions.[2]

The role of the Commission was further spelled out by the objectives stated in the law authorizing the study. Specifically, it was to seek;

— The re-evaluation and improvement of policies for the government to acquire goods and services in a timely, economical, and competitive manner.
— An improvement in procurement organization and personnel.
— The correction of duplication or gaps in laws, regulations, and directives.
— Uniformity and simplicity when appropriate.
— Fair dealing.
— Overall coordination of Federal procurement programs.[3]

As suggested by these objectives, the scope of the study is all inclusive. Both civilian and military purchases are included, unlike previous studies which focused only on military purchases. Procurement organization, the capability of procurement personnel, the policies, regulations, practices, procurement statutes and the leadership functions are also examined. Thus the Commission looked at every facet of how government administers procurement and carries out the process to its final conclusion.

The scope of this chapter must necessarily be more limited. Certain recommendations were selected for discussion because they have a direct impact on marketer strategies. Others have an effect only on certain industries or relate only to the administrative effectiveness of agencies and are therefore not included. However, the study is wide-ranging and insightful in its analysis and therefore every firm marketing to the federal government or contemplating this possibility should obtain and study all four volumes. What the procurement environment for federal contracts in the next several years may be like is indicated by the recommendations.

Need for the Study

The pressure for change in federal procurement came from many points of view. Businessmen complained about the inequities, complexity, and contradictions of various stages of procurement. Procurement personnel complained about the uncoordinated, inconsistent, and voluminous regulations under which they were expected to be efficient. The press made headlines of the cost-overruns of large military purchases for the TFX, Grumman F-15, and Lockheed C5-A aircraft. Despite the fact that dedicated buyers and alert sellers satisfactorily consummated millions of purchases for the government every year, the procurement system was sufficiently inefficient to justify an intensive examination. From this study basis, it would be possible to make significant changes which would save money for the government and facilitate the selling of firms.

Since the principal procurement statutes were passed by Congress, the Armed Forces Procurement Regulations (ASPR) in 1947 for military and space purchases and the Federal Procurement Regulations (FPR) in 1949 for civilian purchases, the procurement process has grown by patch-work solutions to meet the burgeoning needs of government. What was once equitable and satisfactory became, under modified circumstances, inequitable, inefficient, and unduly complicated. By 1965, a myriad of added regulations, policies and directives made it hard for both buyer and seller to be effective. For example, the commission noted this situation:

" . . . a contracting officer at the U.S. Electronics Command, Philadelphia Procurement Division, has a five-foot shelf of procurement and procurement-related regulations which he is responsible for knowing and applying to the extent they govern his area of procurement.

This five-foot stack of regulations does not include interagency regulations such as those of the Department of Labor. Apart from the burden of absorbing and piecing together all this guidance and reducing it to everyday practice, there is the mechanical task of keeping the books up-to-date. Considerable manpower is expended for this purpose alone.[4]

The potential cost savings of the recommendations are significant. For example, if just one recommendation were passed for increasing from $2,500 to $10,000 the limit on exemptions from using advertised procurement procedures for small purchases, the paper-work savings are estimated to be $100,000 annually.

Overview of the Report

The study material gathered by hundreds of investigators was done in study teams. It was gathered in 2,000 meetings around the country and in thirty-six public meetings. Augmented by detailed study and surveys, the original report gathered 15,000 pages of data and opinions from government, business, and academic sources. This has been reduced to four volumes of recommendations and their justifications.

Volume One discusses the general procurement environment including policy and its development, the statutory and regulatory frameworks, changes needed for improvement in the government procurement work force, make-or-buy decisions, and more realistic financing of procurement. Other suggestions deal with cost and profit aspects,the buying of professional services, the implementation of social policies through purchases, and a close look at small business participation in federal contracts. In all, Volume One makes forty-six recommendations and cites numerous other problem areas where improvement is needed.

Volume Two is more specific by centering on the acquisition of research and development, and of major systems such as weapons and space. These two areas are often intimately related, since an R & D contract may lead into or be part of a developing systems purchase. The space shuttle is a prime example of this. Twelve recommendations are made for research and development, and twelve more for major systems.

Volume Three examines the less complicated area of purchasing commercial products and services. Motor vehicles, food, buildings, computers and their programs, and professional services are typical purchases analyzed. Federal grant-type assistance programs which usually purchase services conclude the volume. These areas add twenty-five more recommendations.

Volume Four is similar to Volume One by being broad in scope. Many special issues are included that affect buyer-seller relationships. Problem areas included are the recourse against the parties of the contract in disputes, the matter of liabilities when catastropic accidents occur in connection with contract performance, and the thorny issue of rights in data and patents when firms seek contracts. The remaining fifty-four recommendations relate to these problem areas.

While this chapter deals with only Volumes One and Two, this cursory review of the entire published report serves to expose the significance of all four volumes.

Marketing Significance

Of interest to marketers who sell to federal agencies will be the question, what impact will these Commission recommendations have on the strategies used to seek Federal contracts? Subsidiary to this question is whether the recommendations will increase or decrease the hazards in selling to the government. This will affect the probability of successful performance of contract work. This point of view will be used in assessing the impact of the proposed changes if the recommendations are implemented.

The path of legislation through Congress is arduous. While it is highly speculative to forecast whether the recommendations will be implemented or not, it is reasonable to assume that some procedures will be changed for the better. Certain ones will create lengthy controversy and take considerably longer to change. Principal among these will be the recommended creation of the *Office of Federal Procurement Policy* which would provide a leadership focus for the acquisition process, and the elimination of a multiplicity of procurement statutes in favor of *one statutory basis for procurement* policies and procedures.

Before the recommendations are changed, there is certain to be more discussion in Congress. Before they become law, business firms must use their market surveillance system to be aware of Congressional bills and thereby be alerted to the opportunity to have their viewpoint heard. Constant market feedback will be needed in future years to adapt to this dynamic purchasing environment.

MODIFYING THE BASIC STRUCTURE

The profound importance of changing the basic foundation upon which the Federal government acquires its goods and services makes the first and second recommendations the most wide-ranging in effect and therefore important to firms that seek contracts. The first creates a central office of procurement policy and the second unifies the current statutes into one. These changes and their implications are discussed first. Attention is then turned to the purchase of research and development and of major systems.

Creation of the Office of
Federal Procurement Policy

In the Commissions view, a central group is needed to provide a leadership role for the massive expenditures of the Federal government. This Office of Federal Procurement Policy will provide " . . . an integrated system for effective management, contract, and operation of the Federal procurement process . . . (which would) . . . ensure that procurement operations are businesslike and orderly, and that goods and services are efficiently acquired."[5]

The need for a centralized office is evident in a number of ways. Diverse policies and procedures between Federal agencies disagree about how best to proceed, which creates contradictions, disputes, and inefficiency. In addition, Congress now lacks an orderly feedback mechanism to tell how well the procurement process is proceeding or to obtain coordinating advice on how to improve it. Finally, when agencies are in disagreement, the understaffed Office of Management and Budget (OMB) is the only arbiter available.

With new missions expected of government as the American population grows and international affairs become more complex, it is unlikely anybody can create a procurement organization sufficient for the needs of government ten years from now. A central policy-making group offers a unified way of adapting procurement structure for future needs in an orderly way.

The Office has several objectives. It is to provide instructions and resources to provide a feedback to Congressional committees on how well procurement needs are being met, and to make the needed adjustments in resources so that deficiencies are remedied at the appropriate management level. To do this, a system has been proposed consisting of ten elements:

— The *creation of an Office of Federal Procurement Policy* in the executive branch to assure fulfillment of Government-wide statutory and executive branch requirements in performing procurement responsibilities.

— An *integrated statutory base* for procurement, implemented by a Government-wide regulatory system, to establish sound policies and simplified agency procedures to direct and control the procurement process.

— *Latitude for Federal agencies* to carry out their responsibilities within the framework of Government-wide statutes, policies, and controls.

— *Availability of Funds in time* to permit improved planning and continuity of needed Federal and contractor operations.

— *Government-wide recruitment, training, education, and career development* to assure professionalism in procurement operations and the availability of competent, trained personnel.

— Carefully *planned agency organizations,* staffed with qualified people and delegated adequate authority to carry out their responsibilities.

— A coordinated *Government-wide contract administration and audit system.* The objective is to avoid duplication and deal uniformly, when practical, with the private sector in the administration of contracts at supplier locations.

— *Legal and administrative remedies* to provide fair treatment of all parties involved in the procurement process.

— An adequate *management reporting system* to reflect current progress and status so that necessary changes and improvements can be made when the need appears.

— A continuing *Government-wide program to develop better statistical information* and improved means of procuring goods and services.[6]

The attributes of this central office would include independence of any agency having procurement responsibility, and would have directive authority. It would be answerable to Congress and consist of a small cadre of seasoned procurement experts supported by a staff of experts from areas such as business management, engineering, law, and accounting. Its placement could be within the existing Office of Management and Budget (OMB) which carries the authority of the President.

Perhaps realizing that this recommendation may have difficulty in becoming a reality, the report notes that the other 148 recommendations do not depend on the creation of this central office for their implementation.

A Unified Procurement Statute

The second recommendation focuses on the basic procurement statutes that provide the foundation for government purchasing. Two statutes, the Armed Services Procurement Regulation (ASPR) and the Federal Procurement Regulations (FPR) and many derivative statutes currently exist. These create inconsistencies and in the view of the Commission, unduly complicate the process. Replacing all of them would be one consolidated, up-dated statute which would minimize the need for future amendments.

The desirability of this change can be seen from these situations involving ASPR and FPR:

— *Competitive Discussions.* ASPR requires, but FPR does not, that proposals for negotiated contracts be solicited from a maximum number of qualified sources and that all discussions be conducted with all sources in a competitive range.

— *Truth in Negotiations.* ASPR Requires, but FPR does not, that contractors and subcontractors submit cost or pricing data.

— *Negotiation Authority for Research and Development.* Both acts require agency head approval to negotiate research and development (R & D) contracts. Under ASPR, someone below the head of the agency can approve contracts of up to $100,000. Under the FPR, the limit is $25,000.

— *Specifications Accompanying Invitations for Bid (IFB).*

ASPR states that an inadequate specification makes the procurement invalid. Comparable language is not found in FPR.[7]

From the Commission's viewpoint, no clear reason justifies these inconsistencies which make it more difficult for buyer and seller to transact business. Efficiency, economy and effectiveness would result from a single procurement statute.

Marketing Implications

From the businessman's viewpoint, both of these changes are desirable. First, a central office and unified statute would facilitate the orientation of prospective sellers to the requirements of doing business with federal agencies. It is quite common for a firm to seek contracts from several agencies and as it stands now, each agency with its own modified statute must be studied and dealt with. Secondly, when disputes between buyer and seller or between agencies do occur, a central office could relatively quickly resolve the issue and therefore reduce the need for a court hearing.

On the other hand, changes mean adjustments and those firms accustomed to doing business with government agencies under existing procedures may dislike having to reorient to a new buying environment. Established loyalties may be disrupted and improved surveillance of procurement effectiveness may not be welcomed by all government procurement personnel or business firms. If these recommendations are successful in their goal of simplifying the procurement process, firms presently doing business may find themselves facing increased competition from new firms who may be attracted to government contracts.

Additional recommendations would further refine the procurement statute by making improvements in formal advertising, negotiated procurement, sole-source purchases, and special procurement techniques which reduce barriers to effective buyer-seller interaction. By simplifying government purchasing, the Commission hopes to attract more sellers and for more equitable transactions to result. Therefore the general implication is that more firms will have an opportunity to participate in government contracts, and that the government may reduce its costs in obtaining needed goods and services.

THE PURCHASE OF RESEARCH AND DEVELOPMENT WORK

The Federal government is the single largest purchaser of research and development work in the Western world. Ranging between $15 and $17.8 billion from 1963 to 1972, it represents approximately 7 percent of Federal expenditures for fiscal 1972. Business firms account for 49 percent of this amount with universities, Federally funded research centers, and non-profit research institutions accounting for the rest.[8]

Objectives and Importance

The importance of the R & D area derives from more than the size of expenditures. The governmental dual objectives of supporting this country's technological base and acquiring the capability for producing *new* products and services suggest an even more fundamental importance. Research and development is the well-spring for

FIGURE 10-2
1971 Expenditures for R & D by Agencies*
(Millions of dollars)

Agency	Basic research	Applied research	Development	Total
Dept. of Defense	261.5	1,351.4	5,896.1	7,509.0
NASA	680.3	816.7	1,761.0	3,258.0
Atomic Energy Commission	277.0	152.1	873.9	1,303.0
Health, Education and Welfare	397.3	905.0	173.7	1,476.0
National Science Foundation	272.6	45.7	18.6	336.9
Agriculture	118.4	173.7	12.7	304.8
Commerce	41.8	71.9	30.0	143.7
Housing and Urban Development	0.0	10.5	37.2	47.7
Interior	52.7	86.4	54.7	193.8
Justice	0.0	6.5	3.8	10.3
Labor	2.5	11.1	9.2	22.8
Postal Service	0.0	1.0	38.7	39.7
State Department	0.0	29.0	1.1	30.1
Department of Transportation	0.3	172.8	309.3	482.4
Treasury	0.0	0.4	0.4	0.8
Environmental Protection Agency	6.1	47.7	82.9	136.7
Office of Economic Opportunity	3.2	59.9	90.0	153.1
Smithsonian	15.1	0.0	0.0	15.1
Veterans' Administration	3.1	59.0	0.8	62.9
Other	0.4	17.1	5.2	22.7
Total	2,132.3	4,017.9	9,399.3	15,549.5

*Data rounded

Source: National Science Foundation, *Federal Funds for Research, Development, and Other Scientific Activities*, vol. XXI, tables C-29, C-48, and C-67.

meeting the Nation's continually growing needs for unique, new technology which provide the means for meeting increasingly complex needs. The space program, Polaris submarines, mass transportation solutions, and new generations of aircraft are visible products of this R & D base. Imperfections in the acquisition of R & D work represent a needless impairment of this vital American strength.

This knowledge base is needed by most government agencies. Figure 10-2 illustrates basic and applied research by various agencies in 1971. At the right of the figure are the monies expended for development work which utilizes the ideas from research by creating products and services for specific needs of the country.

The Department of Defense is the largest single user of R & D, requiring almost 50 percent of the 1971 expenditures. Sizable portions are also used by the space program, health, and atomic energy agencies. This reflects the concern the country has faced in the 1960's as solutions are still sought for long-range problems.

Four Areas of Concern

The Commission's recommendations would improve the acquisition of R & D in three major problem areas. Four changes are discussed which would have these effects.

1. They would modify the reimbursability of certain categories of costs which marketers experience in performing this work.
2. They would clarify policies which tend to restrict innovativeness.
3. They would simplify procedural requirements which tend to complicate and delay contracting processes or unnecessarily increase the risk the contractor must bear.

Four problem areas and their recommendations will serve to illustrate how these changes could be effected.

COST ALLOWANCE

In the past, the government has not allowed firms to recover all the costs related to independent research and development (IR & D), bid and proposals (B & P) and various technical costs incident to the work. In other words, firms are expected to absorb a percentage of the cost themselves. This makes firms reluctant to participate unless they think they can recover the costs in further work.

The Commission makes the following recommendation to encourage better relations and induce more firms to do R & D work. Recognize in cost allowability principles that I R & D and B & P expenditures are necessary costs of doing business and that these allowed costs be treated uniformly government-wide. Under certain contracts, the costs are to be accepted as an overhead item without question and reimbursable.[9]

COST RECOVERY

Another point of disagreement has been cost recovery of R & D by the government when the contract results in a salable commodity in non-government markets. In the past, it has been government policy for contracts to have a clause requiring the firm to return a portion of the revenue achieved if the R & D knowledge results in additional products having commercial success. Therefore, if a firm developed a new type of cloth for military uniforms and then found a commercial market for the cloth, a percentage of sales dollars must be returned to the government.

On the face of it, this policy seems logical since public monies helped create the cloth. However, by requiring this stipulation, the government is impairing one of the important incentives firms have for attempting certain R & D work. By reducing this incentive, the government harms itself by occasionally finding itself with no one willing to attempt certain work and if they do, embroiled in cost recovery disputes when firms do find markets for new ideas.

The Commission is blunt in its opinion about this problem: eliminate this recovery cost clause except under unusual circumstances, approved by the governmental agency head.[10] An example of these unusual circumstances would be the development of a new computer or supersonic transport that had a definable market potential beyond government needs such as sales to foreign governments.

HARDWARE EXCLUSION CLAUSES

A third problem area arises from the "hardware exclusion" clause in contracts. In effect, this prohibits the firm from participation in the bidding for the follow-on production contract which will result from the R & D work. The rationale for this is to reduce conflict of interest situations. The effect is to discourage firms from doing R & D and forces the government to choose a supplier who must learn everything the R & D supplier knows. In many cases, this proves to be illogical as well as inefficient.

The Commission recommends that tighter limitations be placed on the use of these clauses. The senior official of the involved agency should rule on each contract whether it is in the larger interests of the country to use the clause or not. When a conflict of interest would occur, it should be used.[11]

COMPETITION FOR CONTRACTS

One of the guiding principles of federal procurement is competition for contracts which should lead to the lowest price for the need as specified. This is achieved with products, but becomes a sensitive problem area when the intangible of research is involved. As the Commission noted, "Identity of product is intrinsically impossible in R & D because of the importance of such qualities as innovation, related experience, and individual qualifications."[12] Uniqueness and innovation in R & D proposals are desired and this has made competitive solicitation of these proposals largely a subjective selection process.

The handling of proposals by agencies has been ambivalent. At times, there has been excessive reliance on sole-source procedures which precludes other firms from offering an innovative approach. On the other hand, when excessively open competition has been used, it results in unnecessarily high costs in payment for proposals. There have been cases where one-hundred proposals resulted from one solicitation requiring the agency to spend months of man-hours to evaluate them. This ambivalence makes the bid, no-bid decision of firms more difficult.

The Commission makes no specific recommendations in this matter, but does suggest a two-thrust position. First, agencies should replace sole source awards with controlled competitive fields with a few competitors in each. Secondly, where many competitors exist and the government is the dominant buyer, stronger selection procedures should be used *before* proposals are solicited, so that weaker firms are eliminated early. One way this might work would be to select the three to five "best qualified potential sources" to prepare a proposal from among those firms interested. An example of how this might work with an aircraft program is illustrated by this situation:

If an R & D program were being planned to investigate advanced wing configurations for Mach 2.5 flight regimes, the qualified bidder list might typically contain 20 or more companies. The "best qualified sources" list would then identify three to five of those who, by virtue of their skills, facilities, and related experience in Mach 2.5 aerodynamics rather than the entire field of aerodynamics, appear to be most suitable. Other applicants would also enter the bidding, provided they feel the effort worth the expense in light of the identified "best qualified sources."[13]

This method would not bar additional firms if they believed they had a superior approach, but it would place them on notice that other firms are considered more qualified at that time.

Implications

The basic meaning of these recommended changes is to open the opportunity for more firms and organizations to do business with the government. By reducing barriers and increasing incentives, the government achieves its objectives of maintaining its vital technological base and reducing the costs of acquiring research and development work.

Specifically, the changes would reduce the disputes between buyer and seller on retrieval of costs and enhance the motivation of firms to seek R & D contracts since they could further exploit technological advancements by finding commercial applications. Firms with both R & D and production capabilities could utilize both if the hardware exclusion clause was used judiciously rather than routinely. This would open opportunity for more firms to do business, as would the reduction in the use of sole source procedures in the placing of R & D contracts.

It frequently happens that R & D work accompanies or is the forerunner of major systems procurement. This is illustrated in Figure 10-2 by the large amounts spent by the Department of Defense and NASA. Many of the conflicts and issues raised about R & D therefore have direct applicability to major systems procurements which is discussed next.

THE PURCHASE OF MAJOR SYSTEMS

Apollo spacecraft, Polaris Submarines, and the C-5A aircraft transport are commonly known household words. These are all major systems. They are means of meeting a need identified by agencies of the government (in this case, NASA and the Department of Defense). Since they are technologically complex and expensive, they are classified as major systems.

No common definition of major systems exists from agency to agency. However, for the purposes of the report, a major system is " . . . a collection of interrelated parts that combine to perform a specific function to meet a national need."[14]

Figure 10-3 illustrates how several existing major systems fit into an overall program. This represents part of the thinking of the Department of Defense for developing and maintaining the military posture of American defense in the five-year defense plan mentioned in Chapter 3.

FIGURE 10-3
Defense Mission Need Hierarchy With Some Specific Related Systems

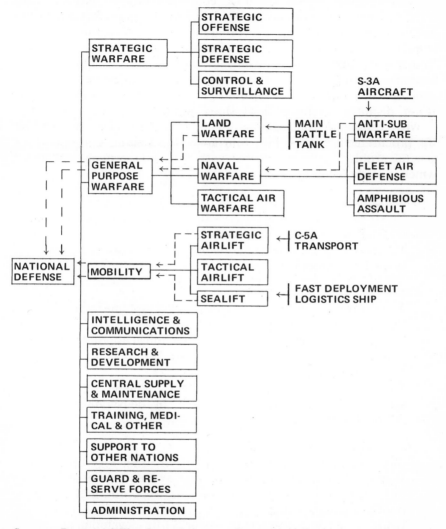

Source: *Report of The Commission on Government Procurement*, Volume 2, U.S. Gov. Printing Office, Washington, D.C., p. 96.

To say that they are vital to the defense and welfare of the country and that they make heavy demands on the money and manpower of the country is to understate the case. In the DoD alone, there are currently 141 major systems representing an investment of $163 billion.[15] Their complexity involves years of work and requires the interfacing of hundreds of firms with dozens of government levels. This complexity and need for integration has been the source of many problems.

Problems Identified

Cost-overruns, contract claims, contested awards, buy-ins, bail-outs, and defective systems are evidence of the imperfections in the procurement of these massive programs. To balance the picture, it should be mentioned that there have been notable successes as well. The space program, ballistic missiles, and the Polaris submarine are examples of major systems successfully made operative. Seeking a procurement process which would create many more successes and fewer disputes is the goal of the Commission. What caused the

What caused the undesirable effects of past systems? By dividing the procurement process into four areas, the Commission cited four general problem areas connected with the DoD systems and about which it made recommendations.

Establishing Needs and Goals
— Needs and goals are set by each military service within the DoD agency leading to unplanned duplication.
— The absence of formal congressional review allowed programs to overlap in missions.

Exploring Alternative Systems
— Too centralized agency-level control over systems reduced the flexibility of management.
— Premature committment to a single technical approach before significant unknown technologies were developed encouraged failures or increased costs.
— Too narrow a technical latitude used for competitors encouraged attempts by firms to "buy-in" by deliverately under-pricing the real cost.

Choosing the Preferred System
— Choosing a firm on paper competition using a complicated source selection procedure. Contract awards became contentious and performance specifications were not met within time and budget limits.
— Using a single contract to cover both development and production where several contracts are needed to realistically set contract costs added to increased costs, disputes, and failures.

Implementation
— Concurrency: overlapping development and production with same results as above.
— Late and inadequate operational tests as a basis for production decisions made agency decisions on awards speculative.

Exploring alternative systems and choosing the preferred system are the areas most relevant to marketer contract strategy. Therefore, the remainder of this chapter will discuss those recommendations which apply to these areas. The other two areas relate more to errors in the decision-making within government agencies and Congress.

Who's At Fault?

It is natural to wonder about who is at fault for these problems. The Commission didn't shirk this question and found fault with nearly everyone connected with the procurement process. They cited marketers, Federal agency heads, agency components, and Congress as contributing to the difficulties.

Congress and its committees spend their time scrutinizing the detail of systems in trying to meet its responsibilities. Its view failed to pay attention to a high order to the responsibility of questioning the justification for the missions or needs, how they intermeshed with past efforts, and the priority to be made in allocating national resources. The broad effects of this lower-level of concern was to disrupt programs and deny the flexibility to those whose responsibility it was to execute the program.

Agency components refer to the military services within the Department of Defense. By reinforcing marketer optimism about contract performance, they encouraged some of their own problems. A desire to meet operational capabilities and to preserve their individual stature and influence were reasons for this behavior.

Agency heads appear to lack adequate control for coordinating their components when faced with severe bureaucratic pressures.

Finally, contractors are sometimes overoptimistic in the cost estimates and their ability to perform. They are encouraged in this by the nature of the selection process and their desire to win a contract award.

To overcome these faults, the Commission makes twelve recommendations. Principal among these is a larger participation by Congress in establishing both the needs and goals and the procedures which acquire the needs of the nation. The discussion will center on defense systems. However, the recommendations are just as relevant to civilian systems.

Finding the Best Approach to a Need

Once Congress and the DoD agree on the priority of the nation's missions, the objective is to find the best system for meeting that need. In the Commission's view, agencies have committed themselves too early to a conceptual approach for meeting a need. In the past, governmental research units, in combination with one or two firms, would develop a conceptual approach and determine the necessary supporting technologies. Then engineering designs were solicited from firms.

This approach tends to limit solicitation of design to large firms who have well-developed engineering capabilities. These firms are well conditioned to the thinking of the agency, which limits their innovation of new concepts. Missing is the smaller firm who may have more innovative concepts for meeting the need, and who has not been restricted in its thinking because of conditioning to the predispositions of agency personnel.

This approach has other unfortunate consequences. Since the system approach has been largely determined, competitors are left with several dubious strategies for attracting the award. These include putting in complicated features uniquely their own, or being overly optimistic about cost and performance dates. Rather than these nuisance differentiations, the Commission feels competitors should be given greater design possibility so that better ideas are generated and competitors can offer a wider spectrum of solutions.

To attract the best ideas available from firms, the Commission suggests four competitive phases for the evolution of a system:[16]

	Basis for Selection
1. *System Conceptual Design*	
This establishes the concept: the operational approach and technologies left open.	Innovative concept and design.
2. *Preliminary Design*	
The system is prescribed, but its main features are left open.	Main design features.
3. *Engineering Design*	
Main design features are now prescribed.	Price and qualitative features.
4. *Production Design*	
Production drawings and design are fixed.	Price

Competition in the first and second design phases have been largely ignored. If competition were encouraged for all phases, then better ideas would be solicited, more firms could compete, and the system would more likely prove fruitful within the estimated time and cost limitations.

In the first design competition, conceptual design, the agency would express only the mission needs, with the firms to innovate an operational approach. All approaches would be carried to following design phases until proven unsound relative to other options. This four-phase approach would widen the technical differences between firms and provide agency heads with a more meaningful choice when deciding on a system.

Choosing the Marketer

When analyzing the major systems where cost-overruns and contested awards have occurred, the Commission noted a recurring situation: Time for deployment of the system was short and perhaps for this reason, the selection of the marketer to create the system occurred while it was still in the paperwork stage. Technologies had not been developed, therefore pricing and performance estimates proved to be excessively optimistic. Added to this is the predisposition of firms to be overly optimistic when they want to attract a contract in order to sustain existing staff and production capabilities.

In high technology systems (for example the C5-A transport, Mark IV torpedo, and Cheyenne helicopter), there are many undeveloped components about which estimates of time and money for development are highly speculative. In addition, the Commission found that in general, the estimating capability of the military services was highly deficient under present circumstances. To reduce cost overruns, contested awards, and disputes, the Commission recommends that competition be used throughout the development period and that the final decision on a system and approach be deferred *until a realistic test of alternate systems can be performed.*

An example of this has already been successfully tried with the "fly off" between Northrup Corporation and Fairchild Industries for the A - X attack plane which is ground support for troops. Fairchild won the contract award after prototype aircraft performed at an air base in California.[17] Under this "fly-before-you-buy" approach, a separate contract for production follows and deals with few unknowns for the firm to estimate cost and time requirements.

The recommendations would require the agency to supply firms with operational test conditions, mission performance criteria, and lifetime ownership cost factors. The latter idea incorporates the well-known "Life Cycle Buying" philosophy of former Defense Secretary Robert McNamara.

Another recommendation does acknowledge that sometimes a

superior approach is known early or that time may be a critical factor for deployment of the system. In these situations, the agency head should designate a strong centralized government management program to see the system to successful completion and select firms with proven capability in the area of technology needed. Cost-reimbursement contracts would be used to assure equity in the risk borne by the firms.

Implications

The recommended approaches greatly reduce the risk firms must currently bear in major systems work. More firms might be more willing to attempt this work if they were more certain of the extent of the risk they would carry if they won a contract. The effect of the near bankruptcy of Lockheed Corporation with the C-5A transport and the large losses of Grumman Corporation on the F-14 fighter aircraft are not lost on other firms.

The Commission would have more competition in the conceptual stage of system design. Smaller firms could participate in systems contracts, whereas in the past, if they participated at all, they participated as a sub-contractor to a large firm who was the principal or prime contractor.

Other implications involve market information. In the past, it has been important for the firm's market information team to be closely tuned to the thinking of the government agency personnel concerned with the system. Under the recommended changes, Congress will become part of the mission evaluation procedure. This makes Congress an even more important group to be studied for information about changes in product requirements, as well as early notification of potential new needs.

SUMMARY

Congress was made aware of wide-spread dissatisfaction with the Federal procurement process in the 1960's and in 1969 created a Commission to intensively study all aspects of government purchasing. A massive study effort resulted in a four-volume statement with 149 recommendations for change. This study will provide the basis for modifications in government purchasing for years to come. This chapter is devoted to those recommendations of the study which would have a direct effect on the marketing strategies of firms if they are implemented.

Three areas of changes are discussed. The first area is the modification of the basic structure for government procurement. The Commission would create an Office of Federal Procurement Policy and eliminate all procurement statutes in favor of one unified statute. The Office would provide a leadership role for procurement by making policy changes when they are needed to coordinate all purchasing activities of various agencies. While both of these changes are for government administrative convenience, their importance to marketers derives from their making Federal markets more equitable, responsive, and in general, easier to deal with.

The second area of change discussed is the purchase of research and development work. The Commission study found numerous practices which made it difficult or undesirable for firms to participate, and made recommendations to remove the disincentives. Specifically, the Commission would allow firms to retrieve all R & D costs, eliminate the requirement that the government receive commissions from commercial sales which resulted from R & D contracts, allow a firm to participate in the follow-on production contract if it desired, and favored a modified selection process for R & D proposals to remove past excesses.

The final area discussed dealt with the procurement of major systems. While many agencies require these systems, the Department of Defense is the most consistent purchaser of high-technology, complex means of meeting a national need. In this area, the Commission maintains that most of the disputes, cost-overruns, and failures can be reduced if more competition is used in the conceptual development phase of system generation, and if simulated competition demonstrations of alternative system approaches are used before the government makes a committment to a systems approach. After a competitive demonstration has demonstrated the superiority of one approach over others, a production contract can be bid with a high probability of satisfactory cost and time performance.

The Commission's recommendations would have the effect of making transactions with Federal agencies more consistent, equitable, and easier to perform for marketers. They will have an effect on the procurement environment for many years to come as agency and Presidential directives, and Congressional laws implement the changes. Some recommendations not requiring a change in law are already being used. It will be important for firms desiring to participate in Federal markets to use their market intelligence capability to be aware of these changes in government attitudes, statutes, policies, and procedures in order to successfully participate in the future.

The rate at which the Commission report recommendations will streamline government procurement is speculative. Pressures from firms, agencies, and within Congress will pull and tug at the recommendations which dramatically change the procurement structure. But change it must, for complaints increase yearly from all parties involved in the process.

FOOTNOTES

1. *Report of the Commission on Government Procurement,* U.S. Government Printing Office, Washington, D.C., 1972. Vol. I, p. 17.

2. Ibid., p. 1

3. Ibid., p. 6 and Section 1, Public Law 91-129. 91st Congress, H.R. 474, November 26, 1969.

4. Ibid., p. 3.

5. Ibid., p. 6

6. Ibid., p. 6

7. Ibid., p. 16.

8. Ibid., Volume 2, p. 12.

9. Ibid., p. 31.

10. Ibid., p. 28.

11. Ibid., p. 47-49.

12. Ibid., p. 43.

13. Ibid., p. 44.

14. Ibid., p. 90.

15. Ibid., p. 89.

16. Ibid., p. 122.

17. "Fairchild Receives A-X Plane Award From Air Force," *Wall Street Journal,* Jan. 19, 1973, p. 5.

QUESTIONS

1. Why is Congress, rather than some other Federal agency, such as the Office of Management and Budget or the President's Office, and logical body to study the Federal Procurement Process?

2. What were the Commission's general objectives? How do they relate to firms who now market to the Federal government? To firms who might enter these markets but are now reluctant?

3. What functions would the proposed Office of Procurement Policy perform which are not being performed?

4. Discuss the advantages to government and marketers of having one procurement statute instead of multiple statutes.

5. What are the problems which inhibit the incentive of marketers to participate in research and development work for the government?

6. What is a major system? What have been the two major errors government has made which resulted in disputes and failures of some past systems? What mistakes do firms make?

7. Using the periodical sources in the library, examine a disputed major system, such as the C-5A or F-14 aircraft. What are the disputes about? What changes are needed to forestall these disputes in the future?

QUESTIONS